SP**OO**N *Spirit*

BLENDER

50 recipes by Catherine Madani

Photography by Françoise Nicol
Consulting Chef Frédéric Vardon

KRUPS COOKBOOK

X | SHAKE | STIR | BLEND

Les Éditions Culinaires

SUMMARY

MISCELLANEOUS VEGETABLES

16

MILKSHAKES

38

MIXED DRINKS
60

SWEET FRAPPES
82

BLENDED DESSERTS

104

SUMMARY

ABOUT THE BLENDER

Modernity
Simplicity
Creativity

These are the three keys to modern cuisine, a seamless blend of day-to-day cooking and holiday feasts, meals with friends and romantic dinners, all of them a pleasure to prepare with the help of a blender.

Modernity

Through the wonders of modern technology, busy modern men and women who love good food and are constantly striving to prepare meals for their families and friends now have high-performance appliances that make it possible to create mouthwatering dishes in the blink of an eye, all while saving precious minutes.

And no appliance is better than a blender at allowing you to easily make not only beverages from around the world, worthy of the most skilled bartender, but also flavorful soups, veloutés that are as velvety as the name implies, chilled potages, and frothy, whipped desserts that draw on the unique abilities of this appliance.

The blender, an elegant but compact appliance, fits naturally into any kitchen, and is always within arm's reach, ready to serve.

Blender Care

Maintenance is never a hassle: the stainless steel blade can be easily removed and washed, and the glass jar is dishwasher safe. What could be simpler?

Simplicity

Nothing beats a blender for simplicity – it is comprised of a motor unit, a jar with a lid, and a metal blade. And while some people consider a blender first and foremost a top-notch drink mixer, it also works wonders with many other mixtures and eliminates the tedious task of using a vegetable mill.

The blender's glass jar, which can withstand sudden changes in temperature, must have a relatively large capacity (60 oz). It can easy handle hot (but not boiling) soups, soft ingredients, and chilled liquids.

The watertight lid includes a measuring cup, making it easy to precisely measure the ingredients for a cocktail or add an ingredient while the blender is running.

The convenience of a blender is not limited to using its high speeds to create perfectly blended cooked soups. It can make batter for crepes, waffles, clafoutis, or even beignets just as quickly.

Starting up the blender slowly prevents splattering. The various speed levels are to be chosen based on the different ingredients used and textures desired. The Varipulse button allows you to monitor the blending and adjust it instantly. And ice cubes crush easily with the special Ice Crush button.

It's easy for anyone to use!

Creativity

The recipes in this book were developed and tested under the direction of Frédéric Vardon, Consulting Chef for the Alain Ducasse Group. Many of them were inspired by the philosophy of the world-renowned Spoon restaurants, whose philosophy is «transparent, multi-cultural fusion of international cuisines.»

Based on familiar classics, these recipes each have a unique twist – from carrot soup with cumin and orange, gazpacho, and sweet piña coladas, to desserts like Fontainebleau with strawberry coulis and raspberry clafoutis; from sweet potato curry velouté, caprese salad appetizers, chocolate hazelnut milk with nut brittle, chocolate custard, and tea-infused crème brûlée, to marshmallow milkshakes, strawberry and tomato soup, and papaya and coconut milk soup. Apart from introducing you to a whole new horizon of tempting treats, these recipes will spark your imagination and inspire you to invent your own original gourmet creations.

HIGH-QUALITY INGREDIENTS

It's no secret. Good cooks insist upon it and anyone who loves gourmet food is well aware of the truth: the success of a recipe depends on the quality of the ingredients. Quality is especially vital for these recipes, since milkshakes, blended drinks, and many whipped desserts call for raw ingredients that are not transformed by cooking.

Achieving this high level of quality requires the careful selection of ingredients (the variety of fruit, the cocoa content of a chocolate, heavier or lighter cream, etc.), and fruits and vegetables at the peak of freshness and maturity, purchased in-season to ensure the best possible flavor.

A few precautions to make sure that your ingredients are top quality ● ● ●

– **Once they are picked, fruits and vegetables start to use up their own reserves,** causing them to lose their flavor and texture. This is why they should be used as quickly as possible. Don't wait too long!

– Remember that **tomatoes lose their flavor when kept in the refrigerator.** Store them at room temperature.

– **Potatoes and zucchinis should also be stored outside of the refrigerator.** They keep well in a dark place that is cool but not cold.

– **Be careful with raw milk:** it must be brought to a boil before use, kept in the refrigerator, and used within 48 hours.

– Whether or not you peel them, **fruits and vegetables must be washed carefully** before use.

– **Drink raw fruit and vegetable juices quickly** to prevent them from oxidizing and losing their intrinsic qualities.

Getting Enough Vitamins

It can't be stressed enough: researchers, nutritionists, and doctors, agree that we need to eat at least five servings of raw or cooked fruits and vegetables per day to stay healthy and get all the vitamins and minerals we need.

Since anything novel is more attractive than an old standard, a blender can be an invaluable tool in this effort, helping to expand the range of possibilities to tarbais bean soup with smoked bacon, mushroom velouté with ravioli, cold roasted red peppers velouté, arugula soup with parmesan chips, herb juice, melon with aniseed, tzatziki drink, strawberry-orange jelly, sweet piña colada, strawberry-tomato soup, and cinnamon-pear soup, just to name a few. The popular milkshake, which comes in a variety of delicious flavors, is another blender specialty, rich in protein, calcium, and the vitamins found in milk, an integral part of any healthy diet.

All these qualities should easily convince children or reluctant adults to eat fruits, vegetables, and dairy products instead of turning them down.

Fortified milk, or milk with a guaranteed vitamin content, is obtained by reintroducing the vitamins lost during the pasteurization or sterilization process into the milk, thus bringing the vitamin content closer to that of fresh cow milk.

To make the best whipped cream, use very cold whipping cream with 30% butterfat.

Presentation

One final point to remember is presentation.

However delicious it may be, any dish should be presented well, because the eyes enjoy a meal before the palate has its say.

So dare to add a splash of color here or a few green leaves there. Take the time to complete your masterpiece with parmesan chips or caramel ribbons. Garnish your glasses with white sugar or, even better, colored sugar. Serve your creations in attractive dishes: bowls, cups, tureens, ramekins, molds in a variety of shapes and sizes, colorful plates, and whimsical glasses that complement your menu, so that your guests can start to enjoy the meal even before they take their first bite.

MISCELLANEOUS VEGETABLES

CARROT SOUP
WITH ORANGE AND CUMIN

GAZPACHO

COLD BEET VELOUTÉ

TARBAIS BEAN SOUP
WITH SMOKED BACON

PEA AND LETTUCE VELOUTÉ

MUSHROOM VELOUTÉ
WITH RAVIOLI

COLD ROASTED RED PEPPER VELOUTÉ

SWEET POTATO AND CURRY VELOUTÉ

CHILI STYLE BLACK BEAN SOUP

ARUGULA SOUP
WITH PARMESAN CHIPS

CARROT SOUP

WITH ORANGE AND CUMIN

Serves 4

6	carrots (about 1 lb)
2	oranges
2	cloves garlic
1 1/4 inches	fresh ginger
1 tsp	turmeric
2 tsp	cumin seeds
1 small	bunch cilantro
4	Petits Suisses (or 2 yogurts)
2 Tbsp	olive oil
	salt

1. Peel and slice the carrots, then drop them into salted, boiling water. Let cook for 5 minutes, then drain.

2. Juice the oranges. Peel and chop the garlic. Peel the ginger and grate it finely. 1 teaspoon of ginger is needed.

3. Heat the olive oil in a deep, thick-bottomed frying pan. Sautée the garlic, turmeric, ginger, and half the cumin for 1 minute over medium heat.

4. Add the carrots and orange juice. Add enough water to cover the carrots. Bring to a boil, cover, and cook for 10 to 15 minutes.

5. Heat the rest of the cumin in a dry frying pan for 1 minute. Wash and dry the cilantro, then chop the leaves with a knife.

6. Pour the contents of the frying pan into the blender. Lock the lid but take out the measuring stopper to allow steam to escape. Pulse together for several seconds. Then increase to speed level 3. If there is not enough liquid, add mineral water to reach the desired consistency.

7. If necessary, reheat the soup for a few minutes. Season to taste. Divide the soup into bowls and sprinkle with cumin and chopped cilantro. Place a Petit Suisse in the center. Serve immediately.

GAZPACHO

Serves 4			
1-1/2 lbs	tomatoes	**Garnish**	
3/4	cucumber	1	tomato
1	red pepper	1/2	red pepper
3	green onions	1	green onion
3	cloves garlic	4 inches	cucumber
2 oz	sourdough bread (1 medium slice)	1 Tbsp	olive oil
1 Tbsp	sherry vinegar	1 tsp	lemon juice
	few drops Tabasco		salt, pepper
1/2 cup	still mineral water		
3 Tbsp	olive oil		

1. Peel the tomatoes, cucumber, and red pepper. Seed them. Chop all the vegetables into pieces. Wash the green onions and chop them into thin slices. Peel the cloves of garlic.

2. Pour half of the vegetable pieces and garlic into the blender jar. Add half of the bread, chopped into pieces, half the vinegar, a few drops of Tabasco, half the olive oil and 1/4 cup mineral water. Salt lightly. Lock the lid. Pulse together on speed level 3. Then increase to speed level 4.

3. When the mixture is smooth, pour the contents of the blender into a mixing bowl. Blend the rest of the ingredients in the same way. Add the contents of the jar to the mixing bowl, stir together, check the seasoning, cover, and leave in the refrigerator for at least 2 hours.

4. Shortly before serving, prepare the garnish: wash the tomato and the half-pepper. Peel and dice them. Peel the green onion. Chop the bulb and tender part of the green stalk. Peel the cucumber, cut it in half, remove the seeds, and dice.

5. Mix 2 teaspoons of each vegetable with 1 tablespoon of olive oil and 1 teaspoon of lemon juice. Add salt and pepper.

6. Stir the gazpacho with a wooden spoon or spatula, divide it into bowls, and place 1 tablespoon of garnish on each bowl.

Be careful not to exceed the limit indicated on the blender jar. It is better to repeat the process than to overfill the jar.

COLD BEET VELOUTÉ

Serves 8	
1-3/4 lbs	cooked beets
1	red onion
1	cucumber
1 Tbsp	cider vinegar
1/2 cup	whipping cream
1	Granny Smith apple
1/2 cup	vegetable stock
	salt, pepper

1. Peel and chop the beets. Peel and halve the cucumber. Remove the seeds from the center using a small spoon. Slice the cucumber. Peel and dice the red onion.

2. Place the prepared vegetables into the blender jar. Add the cider vinegar and vegetable stock. Lock the lid. Blend on speed level 2 and then on speed level 4, until the mixture is homogeneous. Add salt and pepper. Place in refrigerator for 2 hours.

3. Just before serving, peel the apple. Dice it or cut it into thin strips. Pour the velouté into bowls. Add the whipping cream and garnish with the apple.

TARBAIS BEAN SOUP
WITH SMOKED BACON

Serves 4	
1/2 lb	Tarbais beans (or white beans)
1	leek
1 small	stalk celery
1	tomato
4 tsp	butter
3 branches	fresh thyme
50 oz	chicken stock (6-1/2 cups)
8 thin slices	smoked bacon
	Espelette pepper (hot chili pepper)
	salt, pepper

1. Place the beans in a large bowl and cover completely with cold water. Let them soak for 8 to 12 hours.

2. The following day, clean the leek and celery. Cut both into slices. Sauté the leek in the butter for 2 minutes, add the celery, and let the ingredients cook for 10 minutes.

3. Drain the beans and put them into a stockpot with the sautéed vegetables, tomato, and thyme. Add the chicken stock. It must cover the beans by at least an inch. Add mineral water as necessary. Bring slowly to a boil, cover, and simmer for about an hour and a half, until the beans are very tender.

4. After simmering, remove the thyme. Pour half of the contents of the stockpot into the blender jar. Lock the lid, making sure to take out the measuring stopper to allow steam to escape. Blend on speed level 2, increasing to speed level 3. Empty the blender jar into a saucepan. Pour the remainder of the contents of the stockpot into the blender and blend in the same way. Empty the blender jar into the saucepan, season to taste, and reheat the soup over low heat.

5. Heat a non-stick frying pan. Place the bacon in the frying pan and fry each side for 1 minute.

6. Pour the hot soup into bowls. Place 2 slices of bacon on each one and sprinkle with a little Espelette pepper.

PEA AND LETTUCE VELOUTÉ

Serves 4	
5 lbs	fresh peas
1	leek
1 small	head lettuce
1	clove garlic
6	sprigs mint
3	green onions or 1 white onion
34 oz.	vegetable stock (4-1/4 cups)
1/2 cup	heavy cream
2 Tbsp	grated parmesan cheese
2 Tbsp	olive oil
	salt

1. Remove the peas from their pods. Peel, wash, and thinly slice the leek. Peel and slice the onions. Peel and chop the garlic. Clean and wash the lettuce, dry it, and cut it into strips. Rinse the mint and remove the leaves from the sprig.

2. In a large pot, sauté the leek, onions, and garlic in olive oil until the leek is soft.

3. Pour the vegetable stock into the pot. Add the lettuce and peas. Bring to a boil, cover, then reduce the heat and simmer for about 15 minutes, until the peas are tender.

4. Remove the pot from the heat. Add the mint leaves.

5. Pour the contents of the pot into the blender. Lock the lid, making sure to take out the measuring stopper to allow steam to escape. Blend on speed level 4 until the mixture is homogeneous. Season to taste.

6. Just before serving, add the heavy cream and grated Parmesan.

If necessary, blend the soup in two batches to avoid exceeding the capacity of the blender.

Serve this velouté with chicken oyster sautéed with girolle mushrooms and pieces of crispy pancetta.

MUSHROOM VELOUTÉ
WITH RAVIOLI

Serves 4

1-1/3 lbs	mixed mushrooms (girolles, oyster caps, chanterelles, porcini, etc.) or a frozen mixture
3	shallots
3	cloves garlic
1-1/2 Tbsp	butter
3/4 cup	heavy cream
1-1/4 cups	chicken or vegetable stock
1-1/4 cups	milk
2/3 cup	oil for frying
5	sprigs chives
1 pinch	nutmeg
16	fresh herb and cheese ravioli (2cm in size – total 7 oz.)
	salt, pepper

1. Clean the mushrooms. Wash them quickly without soaking them. Do not wash the porcini mushrooms but wipe them with damp paper towel. Cut the mushrooms into pieces. Peel and chop the garlic and shallots.

2. In a thick-bottomed saucepan, melt the butter with the garlic and shallots for 3 minutes, over a low heat, stirring constantly. Then add the mushrooms and brown them for 3-4 minutes over high heat. Season with salt and pepper, and add the nutmeg.

3. Add the milk and stock, bring to a boil, and then lower the heat and leave to simmer 10 minutes.

4. Pour the contents of the saucepan into the blender jar. Lock the lid making sure to take the measuring cap out of the lid to allow steam to escape. Blend on speed level 3. Pour the soup back into the saucepan and heat it again. Stir in the cream and allow to cook for 2 minutes.

5. Heat the oil in a frying pan and add the ravioli. Allow them to turn golden, 1 or 2 minutes on each side.

6. Pour the soup into bowls. Wash and chop the chives, and sprinkle them over the soup. Divide the ravioli among the bowls and serve straight away.

If the garlic is not fresh, cut the cloves in half and remove the green shoot in the middle.

MISCELLANEOUS VEGETABLES

COLD ROASTED RED PEPPER VELOUTÉ

Serves 4

3	red peppers
6	cloves garlic
1/3 cup	whole milk
1 tsp	olive oil
2 tsp	soy sauce
1 Tbsp	balsamic vinegar
	several basil leaves

1. Turn on the oven broiler. Place the peppers on a baking sheet. Place it as close as possible to the broiler and roast the peppers for about 20 minutes, until the skin swells and blackens. Turn them regularly.

2. Place the unpeeled cloves of garlic in a small oven-safe dish, pour olive oil over them, and pour a bit of water into the bottom of the dish. Place the dish next to the peppers. After about 5 minutes, the skin should be grilled and the garlic should be soft.

3. Remove the skin, seeds, and stems from the peppers. Cut them into pieces. Peel the garlic.

4. Place the peppers, garlic, vinegar, soy sauce, and milk in the blender jar. Lock the lid and blend on speed level 4 until the mixture is homogeneous.

5. Pour the velouté into a soup tureen and leave in the refrigerator for at least 2 hours.

Serve the velouté cold, garnished with a basil leaf.

MISCELLANEOUS VEGETABLES

SWEET POTATO
AND CURRY VELOUTÉ

Serves 4

2	sweet potatoes (about 1 3/4 lbs)
1/2 cup	milk
1/3 cup	shredded coconut
3/4 cup	chicken or vegetable stock
1/3 cup	heavy cream
1 oz	chopped hazelnuts or cashew nuts
1 tsp	curry powder
1 tbsp	mango chutney
	juice of half a lemon
	salt, pepper

1. Peel the sweet potatoes and chop into small pieces. Place them in a saucepan. Cover the sweet potatoes with water, salt them, and cook for 15 minutes or until tender. Drain.

2. Pour the milk into a separate saucepan, add the coconut, and heat until the liquid starts to simmer, without letting it boil.

3. Pour the milk and coconut into the blender jar. Add the stock, chutney, curry powder, and lemon juice. Lock the lid and blend on speed level 3 until the mixture is homogeneous. Add the sweet potatoes and increase to speed level 4. Season to taste.

4. Just before serving, reheat the soup, pour it into bowls, add a small amount of heavy cream, and sprinkle with chopped nuts.

CHILI STYLE
BLACK BEAN SOUP

Serves 4			
1/2 lb	black beans	1 tsp	powdered cumin
10 oz	ground beef	4 oz	cheddar or mimolette cheese
2	onions		
2	cloves garlic	2 Tbsp	crème fraîche
2 tsp	chili powder	2 Tbsp	oil
1/2 can	peeled tomatoes		salt
4 oz	sun dried tomatoes in oil		

1. Place the beans in a large bowl and cover completely with cold water. Let them soak for 8 to 12 hours.

2. Drain the beans, place in a large pot, and add enough water to cover them. Bring to a boil, cover the pot, then simmer at a low boil for about an hour and a half, until the beans are tender. Salt 30 minutes before finishing.

3. Peel and slice the onions and garlic. Chop the sun dried tomatoes into small pieces.

4. Heat the oil in a pan and sautée the onions and garlic. When they start to become transparent, add the sun dried tomatoes and the peeled tomatoes. Sprinkle with chili and cumin. Let simmer for 1 minute, then add the meat. Brown for several minutes, stirring and breaking up the meat with a fork. Cook for about 20 minutes.

5. Pour the beans and the water used to cook them, and the contents of the frying pan into the blender jar. Lock the lid, making sure to take out the measuring stopper to allow steam to escape. Pulse together on speed level 2. Then increase to speed level 4 and blend until the mixture resembles a thick soup.

6. Grate the cheese. Pour the soup into bowls, add 1 teaspoon of crème fraîche to each one, and sprinkle with grated cheese.

The meat can also be served as a tartare: season with salt, pepper, Tabasco, onions, capers, and chopped parsley, roll into small balls, and serve alongside the soup.

Blend the soup in two batches to avoid exceeding the capacity of the blender.

Black beans, grown in South America, can be found in gourmet grocery stores.

MISCELLANEOUS VEGETABLES

ARUGULA SOUP

WITH PARMESAN CHIPS

Serves 4

1-1/3 lbs	potatoes
1	onion
2/3 lb	arugula
4 1/4 cups	vegetable stock
1 cup	grated parmesan cheese
2 Tbsp	olive oil
	salt, pepper

1. Peel and wash the potatoes, then chop them into small pieces. Peel and slice the onion. Wash and dry the arugula. Preheat the oven to 425°F.

2. Put the oil in a saucepan and sauté the onion until it becomes transparent. Add the potatoes and vegetable stock. Bring to a boil, cover, and reduce the heat. Simmer for about 15 minutes, until the potatoes are tender.

3. Add the arugula to the potatoes and continue to cook for 2 minutes. Add salt and pepper.

4. Pour the contents of the saucepan into the blender. Lock the lid, making sure to take out the measuring stopper to allow steam to escape. Pulse together on speed level 2. Then increase to speed level 4 until the mixture is homogeneous.

5. Cover a baking sheet with waxed paper. Place the parmesan cheese on it in 4 small piles, and spread the piles slightly. Place in the oven and bake the parmesan chips for 1 to 2 minutes. Remove them with a metal spatula.

6. Reheat the soup if necessary, pour it into glasses or bowls, and serve with the parmesan chips on the side.

MISCELLANEOUS VEGETABLES

STRAWBERRY
AND ROSE WATER LASSI

LEMON CHEESECAKE YOGURT

MARSHMALLOW MILKSHAKE

BANANA
AND TAPIOCA COCONUT MILK   MILKSHAKES

CHOCOLATE SOY MILK
A L'ORANGE

APRICOT ALMOND MILK

CHOCOLATE HAZELNUT MILK
WITH NUT BRITTLE

RASPBERRY MERINGUE MILK

PROTEIN-PACKED BREAKFAST

PEACH EGGNOG

STRAWBERRY
AND ROSE WATER LASSI

Serves 4

1/2 lb	strawberries
4 plain	Greek-style ewe's milk yogurts
3 or 4 tsp	honey
1 tsp	rose water
6	ice cubes

1. Wash the strawberries quickly in cold water, dry them on paper towel, and stem them.

2. Place the ice cubes in the blender jar. Lock the lid. Press the Ice Crush button to crush the cubes.

3. Add the yogurts, honey, strawberries, and rose water. Blend at speed level 4 to obtain a thick, creamy mixture.

4. Divide the lassi into 4 glasses and serve immediately.

Do not let the strawberries soak, as they will absorb water.

LEMON CHEESECAKE YOGURT

Serves 4

2	plain yogurts
1/2 cup	cold whipping cream
3 tbsp	granulated sugar
1/2 cup	Philadelphia cream cheese or Saint-Moret
1	lemon
1/2 tsp	vanilla extract
2 pinches	nutmeg
6	ice cubes

1. Press the lemon. Filter the resulting juice.

2. Place the ice cubes in the blender jar. Lock the lid and press the Ice Crush button to crush the cubes.

3. Add the yogurt, whipping cream, cream cheese, sugar, lemon juice, and vanilla one after another. Lock the lid. Blend on speed level 3 until the mixture is creamy.

4. Divide the mixture into glasses. Sprinkle with nutmeg and serve cold.

Serve the cold yogurt with spice or shortbread cookies and garnish with very fine lemon zest.

Serve with a lightly sweetened berry marmalade.

MILK SHAKES

MARSHMALLOW MILKSHAKE

Serves 4

3/4 cup	cream
2 oz	marshmallows or strawberry-flavored gummy candies
2	plain yogurts
6	ice cubes

For the garnish

1 Tbsp	lemon juice
	colored sugar

1. Heat the cream. Use a pair of scissors to cut the marshmallow into pieces. Dissolve it in the warm cream while stirring. Let cool, strain, and then place in the freezer for several minutes until the mixture is cold.

2. Place the ice cubes in the blender jar. Lock the lid. Press the Ice Crush button to crush the cubes.

3. Add the marshmallow cream and the yogurt. Blend on speed level 4 until the mixture is creamy.

4. Pour the lemon juice into a saucer. Spread out the colored sugar on a second saucer. Dip the rim of each glass in the lemon juice, then in the colored sugar.

5. Pour the milkshake into the glasses without touching the rims and serve immediately.

BANANA
AND TAPIOCA COCONUT MILK

Serves 4

4	bananas
1/4 cup	sugar
2-1/2 cups	coconut milk
1/4 cup	tapioca

1. Pour 2 cups of coconut milk into a saucepan. Bring to a boil. Pour the tapioca into the boiling coconut milk and cook for about 15 minutes, stirring frequently, until the tapioca balls become translucent and swollen. Remove from heat and allow to cool.

2. Peel the bananas and cut them into pieces. Place the bananas in the blender jar with the sugar and 1/2 cup of coconut milk. Lock the lid. Pulse on speed level 2 until you obtain a thin purée.

3. Pour the banana purée into glasses. Then add the coconut milk tapioca. Serve slightly warm.

CHOCOLATE SOY MILK
A L'ORANGE

Serves 4

2 cups	soy milk
6 oz	dark chocolate
1 cup	granulated sugar
1	orange
8 pieces	candied orange peel
6	ice cubes

1. Break the chocolate into pieces, place them in a heat-resistant bowl or double boiler and melt them over a saucepan of simmering water.

2. Pour half of the melted chocolate into the blender jar. Add half of the soy milk. Lock the lid. Blend on speed level 4. Pour the remainder of the soy milk into the blender through the opening in the lid and blend once again on speed level 4. Set aside the chocolate soy milk and rinse out the blender jar.

3. Dip the pieces of candied orange peel one by one in the remaining melted chocolate and place them on a plate covered in waxed paper. Place the plate in the refrigerator for 15 minutes to harden the chocolate.

4. Wash and dry the orange. Use a zester to remove thin strips of the peel. Pour the sugar into a saucepan, add 1/2 cup of water and stir constantly until the sugar has dissolved. Bring to a boil. Lower the heat, drop the strips of zest into the syrup, and let them candy for 5 minutes. Drain them.

5. Just before serving, place the ice cubes in the blender jar. Lock the lid. Press the Ice Crush button to crush the cubes. Stop the blender, add the chocolate milk through the opening, and blend on speed level 4.

6. Pour the chocolate milk into glasses. Garnish with the candied zest and serve with the chocolate-dipped orange peel.

MILK SHAKES

APRICOT ALMOND MILK

Serves 4

2 cups	milk
1 cup	crushed almonds
8 large or 12 small apricots (1 lb)	
1/2 cup	granulated sugar
	several lavender seeds
	several sliced almonds
6	ice cubes

1. Pour the milk, crushed almonds, and sugar into a saucepan. Bring slowly to a boil, remove from the heat, and let steep until cooled.

2. Wash and dry the apricots, pit them, and cut them into pieces.

3. Filter the almond milk using a fine strainer.

4. Place the ice cubes into the blender jar. Lock the lid. Press the Ice Crush button to crush the cubes. Add the milk and apricots through the opening in the lid. Pulse them together on speed level 2, then increase to speed level 4 until the mixture is frothy.

5. Pour into glasses immediately and garnish with the lavender seeds and sliced almonds.

CHOCOLATE HAZELNUT MILK
WITH NUT BRITTLE

Serves 4	
2 cups	milk
1 cup	ground hazelnuts
3/4 cup	whole hazelnuts
1/2 cup	pistachio nuts, shelled
4 oz	baking chocolate
2	scoops vanilla ice cream
2/3 cup	granulated sugar
6	ice cubes

1. Combine the milk with the ground hazelnuts and bring to a boil. Turn off the heat and let steep until cooled.

2. Break the chocolate into pieces, place them in a heat-resistant bowl or double boiler, and melt them over a saucepan of simmering water.

3. Filter the milk. Place the melted chocolate, half of the milk, and 2 scoops of ice cream in that order into the blender jar. Lock the lid. Blend on speed level 2. Pour the rest of the milk through the opening in the lid, then increase to speed level 4. Set the mixture aside. Rinse out the blender jar.

4. Chop the hazelnuts and pistachios into large pieces.

5. Place the sugar in a small saucepan, add 3 tablespoons of water to moisten it, and heat until it becomes a golden-colored caramel. Pour the caramel onto waxed paper and sprinkle it with the hazelnuts and pistachios. Let the nut brittle cool at room temperature.

6. Break the resulting brittle into pieces.

7. Just before serving, place the ice cubes into the blender jar, lock the lid, and press the Ice Crush button to crush the cubes. Pour the chocolate milk through the opening in the lid and blend on speed 4.

8. Serve the hazelnut milk immediately, garnished with pieces of the brittle.

RASPBERRY MERINGUE MILK

Serves 4

10 oz (1-1/3 cups) sweetened condensed milk
1 cup   milk
2/3 lb   raspberries
4 small meringues
10   ice cubes

1. Place the ice cubes in the blender jar, lock the lid, and press the Ice Crush button to crush the cubes.

2. Add the raspberries, milk, and condensed milk through the opening in the lid. Pulse them together on speed level 3 for several seconds, then increase to speed level 4 and continue to blend until the mixture is homogeneous.

3. Crush the meringues into large pieces.

4. Pour the milk into glasses, garnish with pieces of meringue, and serve immediately.

MILK SHAKES

PROTEIN-PACKED BREAKFAST

Serves **4**

2-1/2 cups granola
4 plain or vanilla yogurts
1 lb blueberries
4 Tbsp honey

1. Check that the blueberries are in good shape and have had their stems removed. Rinse them in cool water and dry them using a paper towel.

2. Place the granola and 2 yogurts in the blender jar. Lock the lid and blend on speed level 2 for several seconds.

3. Add the blueberries, 2 remaining yogurts, and the honey through the opening in the lid. Blend together on speed level 2, then increase to speed level 4 until the mixture is homogeneous. Serve immediately.

PEACH EGGNOG

Serves 4

4	ripe peaches
2 cups	ice milk
2 plain	yogurts
3	fresh eggs (preferably organic)
3 Tbsp	honey
1 pinch	cinnamon

1. Peel the peaches, remove the pits, and cut into pieces.

2. Place the peaches, honey, and eggs in that order in the blender jar. Lock the lid. Blend on speed level 2.

3. Add the milk, yogurts, and cinnamon through the opening in the lid. Blend on speed level 4 until the mixture is homogeneous.

Serve cold.

HERB JUICE

MELON WITH ANISETTE

LEMONGRASS
GINGER AND PINEAPPLE SODA

MIXED DRINKS

FLAVORED ICED INFUSION

PEACH AND VERBENA TEA

CAPRESE SALAD APPETIZERS

TZATZIKI DRINK

SWEET PIÑA COLADA

CHERRY SMOOTHIE

ICED PRUNE TEA

HERB JUICE

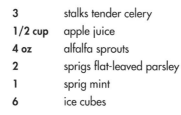

Serves 4

3	stalks tender celery
1/2 cup	apple juice
4 oz	alfalfa sprouts
2	sprigs flat-leaved parsley
1	sprig mint
6	ice cubes

1. Clean the celery with a knife, rinse it, and chop it.

2. Wash the alfalfa sprouts, parsley, and mint, and pat them dry using a paper towel. Remove the stems of the parsley and mint, and chop the leaves into large pieces. One tablespoon of each herb is needed.

3. Place the ice cubes into the blender jar. Lock the lid. Press the Ice Crush button to crush the cubes.

4. Add the celery, alfalfa sprouts (reserving some for garnish), parsley, mint, and apple juice through the opening in the lid. Pulse together on speed level 2. Then increase to speed level 4 until the mixture is homogeneous.

5. Pour the herb juice into glasses and garnish with a few alfalfa sprouts.

SP**O**N
Spirit

Add a drizzle of lemon juice to the herb juice and whisk with olive oil to make a vinaigrette. Use it to season seafood salad or fish.

MIXED DRINKS

MELON WITH ANISETTE

Serves 4

2 small	ripe melons
2 Tbsp	pastis or aniseed-flavored liqueur
1 piece	black licorice
1 cup	still mineral water
8	ice cubes

1. Bring 1 cup of mineral water to a boil. Cut the licorice in two pieces, place it in the saucepan and leave to boil for 2 minutes. Remove the saucepan from the heat and allow the licorice infuse until the liquid is cold. Filter.

2. Cut the melons in half and scrape out the seeds and strings with a soupspoon. Cut the melons into slices, remove the skin, and cut the flesh into cubes.

3. Place the ice cubes in the blender jar. Lock the lid and press the Ice Crush button to crush the cubes.

4. Add the melon, pastis and licorice infusion. Blend on speed level 3 until the mixture is smooth. Serve immediately.

Fruit drinks should be served immediately to prevent them from oxidizing because of their contact with the air.

Pour this mixed drink over small cubes of cucumber, apple, bell pepper, and watermelon, seasoned with salt, pepper, olive oil, lemon, and finely chopped chives for a crunchy soup. Or substitute fruit for the vegetables.

LEMONGRASS
GINGER AND PINEAPPLE SODA

Serves 4

2	limes
1 cup	pineapple juice
1 inch	fresh ginger
3	lemon grass stalks
1/2 cup	granulated sugar
10	ice cubes
1 liter (4-1/4 cups) still mineral water	
2 cups	sparkling mineral water

1. Cut off the ends of the lemon grass stalks and peel off the various layers so that only the tender center remains. Cut the center into pieces. Peel the ginger and grate it finely.

2. Cut the 2 limes in half and juice them. Pour the juice into a saucepan and add the grated ginger, lemon grass, sugar, and still mineral water. Bring to a boil and cook on high heat for about 15 minutes, until about 3/4 of the liquid has evaporated, leaving 1 cup of syrup.

3. Allow to cool, and filter.

4. Place the ice cubes in the blender jar. Lock the lid and press the Ice Crush button to crush the cubes. Then add the syrup and pineapple juice. Blend on speed level 4.

5. Pour equal amounts of pineapple syrup and sparkling water into glasses. Decorate with lemon grass stalks or half-slices of lime.

Keep the ginger root in the vegetable tray in the refrigerator.

FLAVORED ICED INFUSION

Serves 4	
2 cups	still mineral water
6	star anise
1	orange
2	sprigs mint
2 Tbsp	honey
10	ice cubes

1. Wash and dry the orange. Use a zester to remove thin strips of the peel. Press the orange and filter the juice. Wash the mint and remove the leaves from the stalk.

2. Heat the water. As soon as it is simmering, add the star anise and the orange zest. Simmer for 5 minutes.

3. Remove the saucepan from the heat. Add the orange juice, honey, and mint leaves. Let steep until the mixture has cooled. Filter the tea using a fine strainer. Place in refrigerator for 30 minutes.

4. Place the ice cubes into the blender jar. Lock the lid and press the Ice Crush button to crush the cubes. Pour the tea infusion into the blender through the opening in the lid and blend on speed level 4.

5. Pour the tea into glasses and garnish with a few strips of zest and mint leaves, as desired. Serve cold.

SP**O**N
Spirit

This herb tea can be used as a marinade for a tropical fruit salad (sliced mango, papaya, pineapple, kiwi, etc.). Add lemon grass and hyssop juice.

PEACH AND VERBENA TEA

Serves 4

15 g or 3	tea bags verbena tea
2 cups	still mineral water
4	peaches
2	sprigs of fresh mint verbena
2 Tbsp	granulated sugar
6	ice cubes

1. Heat the mineral water, pour it over the verbena tea, and let steep for 8 to 10 minutes.

2. Peel the peaches, pit them, and cut them into pieces.

3. Filter the verbena tea and let cool completely.

4. Place the ice cubes into the blender jar. Lock the lid and press the Ice Crush button to crush the cubes.

5. Add the peaches, sugar, and a little of the tea through the opening in the lid. Pulse together on speed level 2. Then add the rest of the tea and increase to speed level 4.

6. Pour the verbena mixture into glasses. Wash the mint verbena, and garnish the glasses with small bunches of it.

Serve very cold.

MIXED DRINKS

CAPRESE SALAD APPETIZERS

Serves 4

4	ripe tomatoes
2/3 cup	still mineral water
3	basil sprigs
3 Tbsp	olive oil
4	small mozzarella balls
6	ice cubes

1. Remove the skin and stems from the tomatoes. Cut them in half and seed them. Chop the flesh up into small pieces. Rinse the basil. Set aside 4 leaves for garnish. Cut the others with a pair of scissors.

2. Place the ice cubes in the blender jar. Lock the lid and press the Ice Crush button to crush the cubes. Then add the tomatoes, mineral water, basil and olive oil. Blend for a few seconds on speed level 3. Then increase to speed level 4 and blend until the mixture is smooth.

3. Pour the contents of the jar into a container and leave it to chill in the refrigerator for at least 1 hour.

4. Pour the mixture into small glasses. Place a mozzarella ball in each glass and garnish with a basil leaf.

If possible, use buffalo mozzarella, which has more flavor than the cow's milk variety. Balls of mozzarella can be purchased in tubs. Otherwise, scoop four smaller balls from a large mozzarella ball with a melon baller.

Without the mozzarella, this appetizer can be served with a tomato salad or spicy tuna tartare.

MIXED DRINKS

TZATZIKI DRINK

Serves 4	
1	cucumber
2	Greek yogurts (10.5 oz)
2	cloves garlic
3	sprigs fresh mint
1	lemon
6	ice cubes
	salt, pepper

1. Wash the cucumber, cut it into quarters length-wise, remove the seeds with a small spoon, and chop the flesh into small pieces. Wash the mint, remove the leaves from the sprigs and chop them. 3 tablespoons of mint are needed. Peel the garlic and chop it finely or use a garlic press. Press the lemon and filter the juice.

2. Place the ice cubes into the blender jar. Lock the lid and press the Ice Crush button to crush the cubes.

3. Through the opening in the lid, add the cucumber, garlic, yogurt, mint, salt, pepper, and lemon juice. Pulse together on speed level 2. Then increase to speed level 4 until the mixture is homogeneous.

4. Pour the tzatziki into glasses. Garnish with mint leaves and serve cold with pita bread.

To serve the tzatziki as an appetizer dip (with raw vegetables), prepare as directed but omit the ice cubes.

This cool recipe can be served with spicy samosas or as a drink with tandoori chicken.

SWEET PIÑA COLADA

Serves **4**

1	pineapple (1/2 lb)
5 Tbsp	simple syrup
5 Tbsp	coconut cream
juice of **1** lemon + **1 Tbsp**	
10	ice cubes
2/3 cup	shredded, dried coconut

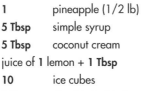

1. Cut off the pineapple leaves and remove the base. Remove the skin using a large knife, like an apple. Remove the eyes with the tip of a paring knife, cut the pineapple into quarters length-wise and remove the hard core. Cut the flesh into small pieces.

2. Place the ice cubes in the blender jar. Lock the lid. Press the Ice Crush button to crush the cubes. Then add the pineapple, simple syrup, coconut cream, and the juice of 1 lemon. Begin pulsing on speed level 3. Then increase to speed level 4 and pulse until the mixture becomes creamy. Add a little mineral water if the mixture is not liquid enough.

3. Pour 1 tablespoon of lemon juice into a saucer. Place the shredded coconut on a small plate. Dip the rim of each glass in the lemon juice and then in the coconut.

4. Carefully pour the drink into the glasses, without touching the rims, and serve.

Coconut cream, which is thicker and richer than milk, is sold in Asian grocery stores.

CHERRY SMOOTHIE

Serves 4

2 cups	cranberry juice
2 scoops	cherry sorbet
1/2 lb	cherries
6	ice cubes

Garnish

sweet popcorn

1. Wash and pit the cherries.

2. Place the ice cubes into the blender jar. Lock the lid and press the Ice Crush button to crush the cubes.

3. Add the cherries, cherry sorbet, and cranberry juice through the opening in the lid. Pulse together on speed level 2. Then increase to speed level 4 until the mixture is smooth.

4. Pour the cherry mixture into glasses and garnish with sweet popcorn.

Make sure that you have removed all the cherry pits, since they could damage the blender.

ICED PRUNE TEA

Serves 4	
2 cups	still mineral water
2	bags Earl Grey tea
8	prunes
2 tsp	honey
10	ice cubes

1. Bring the mineral water to a boil, pour it over the tea, and let steep for 8 minutes.

2. Filter the tea over a cup. Add the honey and stir.

3. Drop the prunes into the tea and let them soak for at least 1 hour.

4. Dry the prunes, saving the tea, and pit them.

5. Place the ice cubes into the blender jar. Lock the cover. Press the Ice Crush button to crush the cubes.

6. Add the tea and 4 prunes into the blender through the opening in the lid. Blend on speed level 4.

7. Pour the cold prune tea into glasses and garnish with a prune on a wooden cocktail stick.

This drink can be served before dinner and seasoned the same way as tomato juice. Prepare the seasoning: bacon, fleur de sel, Espelette pepper (or hot chili pepper), and celery powder.

BLANCMANGER
WITH MANGO COULIS

INDIAN KARDAMOM ICE CREAM

BLUEBERRY DESSERT

ORANGE
AND MANGO POPSICLES

LEMON POPSICLES

SWEET FRAPPES

TOMATO SOUP
WITH STRAWBERRIES AND PEPPERMINT

STRAWBERRY-ORANGE JELLIES

FONTAINEBLEAU DESSERT
WITH CHERRY COULIS

CINNAMON PEAR SOUP

PAPAYA SOUP
WITH COCONUT MILK

BLANCMANGER
WITH MANGO COULIS

Serves 4

1-1/2 cups	crushed almonds
2 Tbsp	almond syrup (or barley water)
6	gelatin packets
1/2 cup	granulated sugar
1 cup	cold heavy cream
2 cups	milk
1	ripe mango

1. Soak the gelatin for 5 minutes in a bowl of cold water. Place a bowl and whisk for whipping the cream in the freezer.

2. Pour the milk and crushed almonds into a saucepan. Bring to a boil, remove from heat, and let steep. Drain the gelatin, wring out the water using your fingers, and add the gelatin to the almond milk while it is still warm. Mix and let cool.

3. Filter the almond milk using a fine strainer. Pour it into the blender jar, along with the syrup and 6-1/2 tablespoons of sugar. Lock the lid. Blend on speed level 4.

4. Pour the cream into the cold mixing bowl, whip until firm, and then fold it carefully into the cold milk. Divide the mixture into ramekins and keep in the refrigerator for at least 3 hours.

5. Remove the mango flesh on either side of the mango pit, remove the skin, and cut the flesh into pieces.

6. Place the mango in the clean, dry blender jar with the remaining sugar. Lock the lid. Pulse together on speed level 2 for several seconds. Then increase to speed level 3, blending until the coulis is homogeneous. Keep the coulis in a cool place.

7. Just before serving, dip the ramekins in hot water for several seconds and remove the formed blancmangers. Serve with the coulis.

SP**O**N
Spirit

Prepare a panful of small mango dice with a split vanilla pod. Cook lightly to keep it slightly crunchy.

INDIAN CARDAMOM ICE CREAM

Serves 4

2 cups	sweetened condensed milk
4	cardamom pods
3/4 cup	unsalted pistachios, shelled
1/2 cup	blanched almonds

1. Toast the almonds and pistachios in a dry non-stick frying pan. When the nuts are golden brown, put them into the blender jar.

2. Heat the condensed milk. Crush the cardamom pods and remove the seeds. Drop them into the milk and cook for 5 to 10 minutes.

3. Let the milk cool slightly and then pour it into the blender jar. Lock the lid. Pulse together on speed level 2. Then increase to speed level 4.

4. Pour the mixture into small ramekins, place in the freezer, and let freeze for 3 or 4 hours.

Remove the frozen cream just before eating. It will not be completely hardened.

Serve this ice cream with a salad made of mint, cardamom, ginger, icing sugar, and olive oil.

BLUEBERRY DESSERT

Serves 4

1-1/2 cups heavy cream
1 lb blueberries
1/3 cup granulated sugar

1. Place the heavy cream, the mixing bowl and whisk into the freezer so that they will be very cold.

2. Wash and dry the blueberries and remove the small stems, if necessary. Place the fruit into a saucepan along with the sugar and cook for about 10 minutes. Let cool.

3. Pour half of the cooked blueberries into the blender jar. Lock the lid and pulse together on speed level 2 to reduce the fruit to a purée.

4. Pour the cream into the cold mixing bowl. Whip, slowly at first and then, when the cream begins to increase in volume, increase the speed. Continue to whip until the cream is quite firm.

5. Very carefully fold the blueberry purée and the remaining blueberries into the whipped cream using a soup spoon.

6. Divide the mixture into small dishes or glasses. Serve immediately.

ORANGE AND MANGO POPSICLES

Serves 4	
2	mangoes
3	blood oranges
1/4 cup	granulated sugar
	flat wooden or plastic popsicle sticks

1. Cut the mangoes on each side of the pit in the middle. Peel the mangoes and cut the flesh into pieces.

2. Cut the oranges in half and juice them. Filter the juice to remove seeds and pulp.

3. Place the mango in the blender jar with the sugar and half of the orange juice. Lock the lid. Pulse on speed level 2. Then increase the speed level until the mixture becomes a smooth coulis.

4. Pour the mango mixture and the rest of the orange juice into small glasses or popsicle molds. Leave for at least 6 hours in the freezer. Place the sticks in the glasses after they have been in the freezer for about 30 minutes.

5. To remove the popsicles from the molds, dip them in hot water for 10 seconds maximum.

Use small narrow glasses, such as vodka glasses. Do not fill them any higher than 1/2 inch from the brim.

LEMON POPSICLES

2	lemons
1 cup	powdered sugar
2 cups	sparkling water
	flat wooden or plastic popsicle sticks

1. Juice the 2 lemons. Filter the juice.

2. Pour the lemon juice into the blender jar. Add the powdered sugar. Lock the lid. Blend on speed level 4 until the sugar has dissolved.

3. Remove the lid, add the sparkling water, and immediately pour the mixture into popsicle molds. Place in the freezer and let freeze for at least 6 hours. Place the sticks in the molds after they have been in the freezer for about 30 minutes.

To remove the ice pops, dip the molds in hot water for 10 seconds.

SWEET FRAPPES

TOMATO SOUP

WITH STRAWBERRIES AND PEPPERMINT

Serves 4

1/2 lb	tomatoes
1 lb	wild strawberries
1/4 cup	granulated sugar
	peppermint leaves

1. Peel the tomatoes. Quarter and seed them.

2. Wash the strawberries quickly. Dry them using paper towel and remove the stems.

3. Place the tomatoes, half the strawberries, and the sugar into the blender jar. Lock the lid. Pulse together on speed level 2. Then increase to speed level 4 until the mixture is homogeneous. Keep in a cool place.

4. Just before serving, cut the remaining strawberries in half, divide them among the dishes, and pour the soup over them. Garnish with peppermint leaves.

Serve with thin finger slices of brioche French toast decorated with thin strawberry slices.

SWEET FRAPPES

STRAWBERRY-ORANGE JELLIES

Serves 4

1 lb	strawberries
6/7	juice oranges
2/3 cup	granulated sugar
8	gelatin packets

1. Soak the gelatin in a bowl of cold water.

2. Press the oranges and filter the juice. You will need 2-1/2 cups of juice.

3. Wash the strawberries. Dry using paper towel and remove the stems.

4. Place the strawberries into the blender jar with 1/2 cup of orange juice. Lock the lid. Blend on speed level 2.

5. Heat the remainder of the orange juice (2 cups) with the sugar. Bring to a boil and remove from the heat. Drain the gelatin, wring it out using your fingers, and add it to the warm orange juice. Mix and let cool.

6. Pour the orange syrup into the blender with the strawberry mixture and blend on speed level 4.

7. Pour the mixture into small, individual molds or ramekins. Let set in the refrigerator for at least 4 hours.

8. Just before serving, dip the ramekins in hot water for 10 seconds and remove the formed jellies onto plates.

FONTAINEBLEAU DESSERT

WITH CHERRY COULIS

Serves 4

1/2 lb	spice cookies
4 Tbsp	butter (softened)
1 cup	very cold heavy cream
2/3 cup	granulated sugar
9 oz	fromage blanc
1 tsp	liquid vanilla extract
1 lb	fresh or frozen cherries
1/4 cup	sliced almonds
4	maraschino cherries

1. Place a bowl and mixer blades in the freezer. Toast the almonds in a dry frying pan, stirring regularly.

2. Crush the cookies into a powder using a food processor or a rolling pin. Mix them with the softened butter. A dry paste should form.

3. Place the fromage blanc, 1/2 cup of sugar, and vanilla extract in the blender jar. Lock the lid. Blend on speed level 3. Empty the blender into a mixing bowl. Rinse out the blender jar.

4. Pour the very cold cream into the cold mixing bowl. Whip the cream until it is quite firm. Fold it carefully into the fromage blanc.

5. Wash the cherries and dry them using a paper towel. Remove the pits. Place the cherries in the blender jar along with the remaining sugar. Lock the lid. Pulse together on speed level 2. Then increase to speed level 4 to make a coulis.

6. From bottom to top, place layers of cookie crumbs, fromage blanc, and cherry coulis into each glass. Garnish with toasted almonds and maraschino cherries.

SPOON
Spirit
For a stronger cherry flavor, add slightly sweetened, highly concentrated cherry marmalade and a drizzle of lemon juice.

SWEET FRAPPES

CINNAMON PEAR SOUP

Serves 4

4	ripe, juicy pears
1/2	lemon
1/2 tsp	cinnamon powder
2 Tbsp	maple syrup
4	slices gingerbread
10	ice cubes

1. Peel the pears, core them, and cut them into pieces. Juice the half lemon. Filter the juice.

2. Place the ice cubes into the blender jar. Lock the lid and press the Ice Crush button to crush the cubes.

3. Place the pears, lemon juice, cinnamon, and maple syrup into the blender jar. Pulse together on speed level 2. Then increase to speed level 4 until the mixture is homogeneous.

4. Slice the gingerbread cake into 1 inch-thick strips.

5. Serve the dessert cold, with the gingerbread strips on the side.

Alternately, rather than cutting the spice bread into strips, crumble 2 slices and brown them in a frying pan with 1 tablespoon of butter for 3 minutes. Sprinkle the crumbled gingerbread cake over the soup.

Make a pear-honey-ginger condiment. Cut the pears into pieces, brown them in a pan with butter, add a bit of honey and chopped-up ginger. Cook to a compote.

PAPAYA SOUP
WITH COCONUT MILK

Serves 4	
1	papaya
1 3/4 cups	coconut milk
1	lime
1/3 cup	granulated sugar
1/4 cup	shredded coconut
8	ice cubes

1. Cut the papaya in half and remove the black seeds with a spoon. Remove the skin from the fruit and dice the flesh. Press the lime and filter the juice.

2. Place the ice cubes into the blender jar. Lock the lid and press the Ice Crush button to crush the cubes.

3. Place the papaya pieces, coconut milk, lime juice, and sugar into the blender. Pulse together on speed level 2. Then increase to speed level 4 until the mixture is smooth.

4. Pour the soup into bowls or glasses, sprinkle with shredded coconut, and serve cold.

TEA CRÈME BRÛLÉE

STAR ANISE CUSTARD

FLAVORED CRÊPES

RASPBERRY CLAFOUTIS

BLENDED DESSERTS

FIG WAFFLES

PANCAKES WITH CITRUS SALAD

PINEAPPLE FRITTERS

CHOCOLATE CUSTARD

ALMOND-ORANGE TUILE COOKIES

CHOCOLATE-MOCHA PARFAIT

TEA CREME BRULEE

Serves 4	
7 oz	whole milk
1 1/4 cup	heavy cream
5	egg yolks
1/4 cup	granulated sugar
2	tea bags (Earl Grey, Darjeeling, jasmine, etc.)
4 Tbsp	brown sugar

1. Preheat the oven to 225°F.

2. Heat the milk until it simmers. Add the tea bags, stir, and remove from heat. Let steep for at least 5 minutes. Remove the tea bags.

3. Pour into the blender jar: the egg yolks, granulated sugar, cream, and milk. Lock the lid and blend on speed level 3 until the mixture is homogeneous.

4. Divide the mixture into 4 crème brûlée dishes. Place into the oven and bake for about 1 hour.

5. Remove the dishes from the oven, let cool, and place them in the refrigerator for about 6 hours. They should be cold.

6. Just before serving, turn on the oven broiler. Dust each dish with brown sugar. Place them in the oven as close as possible to the broiler for about 2 minutes or until the sugar melts and caramelizes. Serve immediately.

SP**O**N
Spirit

You'll be surprised if you use jasmine tea. Serve the crème brûlée with a small slice of brioche French toast sweetened with brown sugar.

STAR ANISE CUSTARD

2 cups	milk
6	star anise
4	eggs
5 Tbsp	brown sugar
1/2 cup	granulated sugar

1. Pour the milk into a saucepan with the anise stars. Bring to a boil. Remove the saucepan from the heat and let steep until cool.

2. Preheat the oven to 350°F.

3. Filter the cooled milk. Break the eggs one by one into the blender jar. Add the brown sugar. Lock the cover. Blend on speed level 3. Pour the milk through the opening in the lid and increase to speed level 4, blending until the ingredients are well mixed.

4. Pour the custard into ramekins. Place them in the oven on the bottom shelf, with a dish of warm (but not boiling) water on the middle shelf, and bake for about 30 minutes. Check for doneness: the custards should be set when a knife can be inserted and removed cleanly. Let cool and then place the custards in the refrigerator for at least 1 hour.

5. While the custards are in the refrigerator, pour the granulated sugar into a small saucepan with 3 tablespoons of water. Cook until the mixture becomes a golden-colored caramel. Pour the caramel onto waxed paper, forming curls. Let dry, then remove carefully.

6. Just before serving, place the caramel curls on top of the custards.

FLAVORED CRÊPES

Makes around twenty crêpes

1-1/2 cups flour
2 eggs
2 cups milk
1/4 cup butter + approx. **1/4 cup** for cooking
1 Tbsp orange blossom water or 1/2 tsp vanilla essence
granulated sugar for sprinkling

1. Melt 1/4 cup butter over a very low heat, then allow to cool.

2. Break the eggs into a bowl and pour them into the blender jar. Add the milk, melted butter, and orange blossom water or vanilla. Lock the lid. Blend on speed level 4 for a few seconds.

3. Pour the flour through the opening in the lid while the blender is running on speed level 3. Pour the batter out into a large bowl, cover and leave to rest for at least 30 minutes.

4. Melt the butter for cooking the crêpes. Heat an 8-inch frying pan. Butter it with a pastry brush. Stir the batter. Pour a ladleful of batter into the frying pan and roll the pan around so that the mixture spreads out evenly. Allow to cook for 1 minute on high heat. Turn the crêpe over and cook the other side for another minute. Slip the crêpe onto a warm plate.

5. Cook the rest of the crêpes in the same way. Butter the frying pan between each crêpe.

6. When all the crêpes have been cooked, fold them into quarters, sprinkle them lightly with sugar and serve immediately.

You can vary the flavor of the crêpes by adding different food flavorings in the mixture (almond, pistachio, orange, etc.).

BLENDED DESSERTS

RASPBERRY CLAFOUTIS

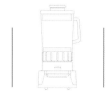

Serves 4

1 lb	raspberries
1/4 cup	cornstarch
2 cups	granulated sugar
2 tsp	vanilla extract
2	eggs + 2 yolks
1 cup	heavy cream
1 cup	milk
1 Tbsp	butter
1 pinch	salt

1. Preheat the oven to 400°F. Butter a ceramic baking dish. Dust it with 1 tablespoon of granulated sugar. Spread the raspberries out over the bottom of the baking dish.

2. Pour the eggs and yolks into the blender jar. Lock the lid and blend on speed level 3.

3. Add the cornstarch, vanilla extract, salt, and the rest of the granulated sugar through the opening in the lid and continue to blend on the same speed level. Add the cream and milk, and increase to speed level 4 to obtain a liquid batter.

4. Carefully pour the mixture over the raspberries. Place in the oven and bake for 35 to 40 minutes. Let cool before serving.

FIG WAFFLES

Serves 4

For the batter

3	eggs
2-1/2 cups	flour
1/2	packet of yeast
2 tsp	vanilla extract
2 cups	milk
1 pinch	salt
4 tsp	butter

For the garnish

8	Violette de Bordeaux figs
4 tsp	butter
1/2 cup	creme de cassis

1. Prepare the batter: break the eggs into a bowl and pour them into the blender jar. Add the milk, sugar, and salt. Lock the cover. Blend on speed level 4. After a few seconds, add the flour and yeast through the opening in the lid, and continue to blend until the mixture is homogeneous and smooth.

2. Melt the butter. Use a brush to lightly coat the waffle iron with the melted butter. Heat the waffle iron. Pour some batter into it and cook for 3 to 4 minutes. Remove the waffle and cook the rest of the batter in the same way.

3. While the waffles are cooking, wash the figs, remove the stems, and cut the figs in halves or quarters. Heat the butter with the creme de cassis in a large frying pan. Place the figs in the frying pan and cook for 5 minutes over high heat, turning them carefully.

4. Place a waffle on each plate and divide the creme de cassis-soaked figs on top of each. Serve immediately.

Pears may be substituted for figs.

PANCAKES WITH CITRUS SALAD

Serves 4

For the batter

2 cups	self-rising flour
1/3 cup	granulated sugar
2	eggs
1-1/4 cups	milk
1-1/2 tbsp	butter

For the citrus salad

2	limes
4	oranges
2	pink grapefruits
1	vanilla bean
or 1 tsp	vanilla extract
2 tbsp	liquid honey

1. Prepare the batter: break the eggs into a bowl and pour them into the blender jar. Pour in the sugar and milk. Lock the lid. Blend on speed level 4. After several seconds, add the flour through the opening in the lid and continue to blend on speed level 3 until the mixture is smooth. Let the batter rest for 15 minutes.

2. Cook the pancakes: lightly butter a small frying pan and heat it. Stir the batter, pour a small ladleful into the frying pan, and cook each side for 1 minute. Remove the pancake and cook the rest of the batter in the same way, lightly buttering the pan before each pancake. Keep the pancakes warm by placing them in the oven on very low heat.

3. Wash 1 orange and 1 lemon under running water, dry them, and use a zester to remove thin strips of their peel. Peel all of the fruit down to the flesh (cutting into the pulp). Remove the sections by running a very sharp knife between the pulp and the white membrane, working over a bowl to catch the juice that drips off.

4. Rinse out the blender jar. Pour the collected citrus juice, honey, and vanilla bean or vanilla extract into the blender jar. Lock the lid and blend on speed level 4 until well mixed. Pour the mixture over the citrus sections and decorate with the zest.

5. Serve the pancakes warm with the citrus salad.

PINEAPPLE FRITTERS

Serves 4	
1	pineapple
1 cup	flour
1	egg
2/3 cup	milk
1 Tbsp	oil
1 pinch	salt
	oil for frying
	confectioners' sugar

1. Break the egg into a bowland pour it into the blender jar with the milk, oil, and salt. Lock the cover. Blend on speed level 4 for several seconds to mix the ingredients. Pour the flour through the opening in the lid while continuing to blend on speed level 3 to obtain a smooth batter for coating. Let the batter rest for 1 hour in a cool place.

2. Cut off the base and crown of the pineapple, remove the skin, and carefully remove all of the eyes with a paring knife. Cut the pineapple into round 1/4-inch slices. Remove the hard core with an apple corer.

3. Heat the frying oil to 350°F. Stir the fritter batter. Dip the pineapple slices in the batter one by one with a small fork. Let the excess batter drip off for several seconds. Place the coated slices in the hot oil and cook for about 3 minutes. Turn the slices over halfway through the cooking time.

4. Pat the fritters dry with a paper towel, place them on a plate, dust with powdered sugar, and serve immediately.

SP**O**N
Spirit

Prepare a spicy pineapple marmalade – with cardamom, red hot chili, honey, and ginger – to dip the fritters in.

BLENDED DESSERTS

CHOCOLATE CUSTARD

Serves 6

8 oz	dark chocolate (60% cocoa)
2 cups	milk
5	egg yolks + **1** egg
2 Tbsp	crème fraîche
1/4 cup	granulated sugar
1 package	of chocolate-covered cookies (see photo)

1. Preheat the oven to 350°F.

2. Chop the chocolate using a large knife. Heat the milk and drop the chocolate into it.

3. Place the egg yolks and the egg into the blender jar. Add the sugar. Lock the lid and blend on speed level 3 for several seconds. Pour the crème fraîche and the chocolate milk through the opening in the lid, and increase to speed level 4 to obtain a homogeneous mixture.

4. Pour the mixture into ramekins or heat-resistant glass dishes. Cover the bottom of a cookie sheet with a small amount of water. Place the ramekins in the cookie sheet and bake for about 30 minutes in the oven.

5. Let the custards cool and then place them into the refrigerator for at least 1 hour.

6. Just before serving, garnish them with chocolate-covered cookies.

ALMOND-ORANGE TUILE COOKIES

Serves 4

1/4 lb	sliced almonds
1	orange
1 cup	flour
3/4 cup	granulated sugar
1 tsp	vanilla extract
5 Tbsp	butter
3	egg whites
1 pinch	salt

1. Preheat the oven to 350°F. Line a cookie sheet with waxed paper. Melt the butter. Wash the orange, dry it, and zest its peel finely.

2. Pour the melted butter into the blender jar. Add the granulated sugar, vanilla extract, and flour. Lock the lid and blend on speed level 3 until the mixture is homogeneous. Pour into a mixing bowl.

3. Add a pinch of salt to the egg whites and beat until they form soft peaks.

4. Use a wooden spoon to carefully fold the orange zest, almonds, and egg whites into the mixture.

5. Spoon small piles of dough, about the size of a walnut, onto the cookie sheet, making sure to leave space between them. Flatten them with the back of a wet spoon. Place them in the oven and bake for about 10 minutes.

6. As soon as the cookies are lightly browned, take the cookie sheet out of the oven. Remove the cookies carefully from the sheet using a spatula and place them on a rolling pin or an empty bottle to give them a rounded shape. Let cool.

Keep the cookies in a dry place in an airtight container.

BLENDED DESSERTS

CHOCOLATE-MOCHA PARFAIT

Serves 4

8 oz   dark chocolate (60% cocoa)
1-3/4 cups heavy cream
3   egg yolks
1 small cup strong coffee (1/4 cup)
           chocolate shavings

1. Place a bowl and mixer blades in the freezer. Chop the dark chocolate finely using a large knife. Boil half of the cream and pour it over the chocolate. Mix gently with a spatula.

2. Place the egg yolks into the blender jar. Lock the lid and blend on speed level 3 for several seconds.

3. Pour the coffee through the opening in the lid and then add the warm chocolate and cream. Increase to speed level 4 to obtain a homogeneous mixture. Empty the blender jar into a mixing bowl.

4. Pour the remainder of the cream into the cold bowl and beat until firm. Mix it carefully into the contents of the mixing bowl.

5. Divide the parfait into small individual dishes or pour it into a cake pan. Leave in the freezer for at least 4 hours.

6. To serve, remove the parfait from its mold, place it on plates, and garnish with chocolate shavings.

Serve with a warm chocolate-cardamom sauce for a warm-cold contrast.

BLENDED DESSERTS

Our heartfelt thanks to everyone who played such an enthusiastic part in putting together this first Krups cookbook, especially:

our colleagues at Groupe SEB, particularly Laetitia Ducout,
Françoise Nicol, for her new gourmet photographs,
Catherine Madani, for her delicious recipe ideas and their consistently appealing presentation,
Elisa Vergne, who deftly adapted the 50 recipes in this book and made them practical,
Anne Chaponnay, for her harmonious page layouts,
Frédéric Vardon, for his culinary creativity,
Textra, Evelyne Strechinsky and Lisa Molle for their translations.

We also thank the following companies:

La chaise longue pp.18, 48
Montgolfier pp. 20, 24, 116
Conran shop pp. 20, 24, 50
Jars chez la maison de brune p.22
La maison de brune pp. 26, 30, 34, 28, 58
Quartz pp. 30, 106
Sentou pp. 32, 40, 114, 102
Deshoulières p.34
Asa p.108
Itinéraires p.48
A. thurpault p.44
Porcelaine virebent pp. 66, 72, 86
CFOC p.72

for lending their plates, cutlery etc.

Collection Editors

Hélène Picaud and Emmanuel Jirou-Najou

Photographs : Françoise Nicol (except for Food Processor photo on cover page: Open Studio Photo; and page 9: Félix Création)
Illustrations: Felix Création
Graphic design and DTP: Anne Chaponnay
Proofing: Isabelle Cappelli

Photo engraving: Maury Imprimeur

Printed in CE
Legal deposit March 2007
ISBN : 2-84123-122-4
ISBN 13: 978-2-84123-122-5

Copyright Lec. 2006
Lec-Les Editions Culinaires
84, avenue Victor Cresson 92441 Issy-les-Moulineaux cedex, France
T: +33 (0) 01 58 00 21 95 – lecedition@wanadoo.fr – www.alain-ducasse.com

Distributed in North America by
Stewart, Tabori & Chang
An imprint of Harry N.Abrams
115 West 18th Street
New York, NY 10011
www.stcbooks.com

Black Americans of Achievement

LEGACY EDITION

Maya Angelou

POET

Black Americans of Achievement

LEGACY EDITION

Muhammad Ali

Maya Angelou

Josephine Baker

Johnnie Cochran

Frederick Douglass

W.E.B. Du Bois

Marcus Garvey

Savion Glover

Alex Haley

Jimi Hendrix

Langston Hughes

Jesse Jackson

Scott Joplin

Coretta Scott King

Martin Luther King, Jr.

Malcolm X

Bob Marley

Thurgood Marshall

Jesse Owens

Rosa Parks

Colin Powell

Chris Rock

Sojourner Truth

Harriet Tubman

Nat Turner

Booker T. Washington

Oprah Winfrey

Black Americans of Achievement

LEGACY EDITION

Maya Angelou

POET

Vicki Cox

CHELSEA HOUSE
PUBLISHERS
An imprint of Infobase Publishing

Maya Angelou

Chelsea House
An imprint of Infobase Publishing
132 West 31st Street
New York NY 10001

Library of Congress Cataloging-in-Publication Data
Cox, Vicki.
   Maya Angelou : poet / Vicki Cox.
       p. cm.—(Black Americans of achievement : legacy edition)
   Includes bibliographical references and index.
   ISBN 0-7910-9224-0 (hardcover)
   1. Angelou, Maya—Juvenile literature. 2. Authors, American—20th century—Biography—
Juvenile literature. 3. African American women civil rights workers—Biography—Juvenile
literature. 4. Women entertainers—United States—Biography—Juvenile literature.
5. African American authors—Biography—Juvenile literature. I. Title. II. Series
   PS3551.N464Z56 2006
   818′.5409—dc22   2006020615

Series and cover design by Keith Trego, Takeshi Takahashi

Printed in the United States of America

Bang Hermitage 10 9 8 7 6 5 4 3 2 1

This book is printed on acid-free paper.

Contents

The Double Dog Dare

Maya Angelou folded her six-foot body down to sit at her mother's kitchen table. Reluctantly, she looked at the ballpoint pen and pad of yellow legal paper in front of her.

She did not want to tell the story of her life. She had told the New York book editor who suggested the idea that she was not interested. She was busy writing poetry and a television series. The editor, Robert Loomis, called her several times. She turned him down after each conversation. Then he threw down a double dog dare that Angelou could not ignore.

He told her, "I'm rather glad you decided not to write an autobiography because to write an autobiography, as literature, is the most difficult thing anyone can do."

Angelou still remembers what happened next. "I said, 'I'll do it.'... The minute someone says I can't, all my energy goes up and I say, 'What? What?'"

Then 40 years old, the singer, dancer, civil-rights activist, poet, playwright, and mother picked up the pen and wrote the first lines of her autobiography:

What you looking at me for?
I didn't come here to stay.

From that moment, Angelou focused all of her attention on telling little Marguerite Johnson's story. She locked her door and started writing. Her friends had to remind her to eat.

When she was finished, she had created more than a listing of the facts about her life from age 3 to 17. She wrote from the inside out. She confessed her inner fears that she did not belong anywhere or to anyone. She revealed her longing to be blonde, blue-eyed, and pretty. She described the people she lived with and the events that happened in their lives. She put faces and places to life as an African American knew it in the Deep South, the Midwest, and California in the 1920s, 1930s, and 1940s.

IN THE SOUTH

Marguerite (Maya) was sent by her parents, who were in the midst of a divorce, to live with her father's mother in Stamps, a racially segregated town in Arkansas.

The center of Maya's Arkansas world was the Wm. Johnson General Merchandise Store. It was the only black store in town, and her grandmother, Annie Henderson, owned it. Maya and her brother, Bailey, helped their grandmother, or Momma as she was soon called, and their Uncle Willie. They worked in the store, selling crackers, pickles, flour, and cloth to the African Americans who lived on their side of Stamps.

In her autobiography, Angelou made readers see and smell and hear what she saw and smelled and heard in that store. She described the bare wooden floors, the shelves of canned goods, and the odors of oranges, onions, and kerosene mixing in the air.

During the season, little Maya waited on the pickers who came to the store, dragging their empty cotton sacks across the floor to buy peanut paddies, cans of sardines, or "sody crackers" for their lunch. They returned in the evening, their fingers cut by the cotton's hulls. Angelou remembered that they were "turned gray" by the cotton lint and dust in their hair: "The women's feet had swollen to fill the discarded men's shoes they wore."

It was there, in the store's carrot and onion bin, that Momma hid Uncle Willie from the Ku Klux Klan. The gang of whites hooded their heads with only their "eyes of hate" showing as they beat, maimed, or killed blacks.

It was just outside the store that Maya watched helplessly as "powhitetrash" girls insulted and mocked an adult, her dignified grandmother, just because their skin was white and hers was black.

MOMMA AND BAILEY

Momma was the most important adult in young Maya's life. Angelou later wrote, "I saw only her power and strength. She was taller than any woman in my personal world and her hands were so large they could span my head from ear to ear." Angelou wrote with pride that Momma was the only African American in Stamps whom white people had addressed as "Mrs." Momma was a successful businesswoman. White sharecroppers rented land from her. During the Depression, she lent money to a white dentist. She even figured out a way for her customers to trade their government-issued relief supplies— lard, flour, salt, powdered eggs, and milk—for the store's sugar, peanut butter, and laundry soap.

Momma's morals were as stiff as her starched aprons. She insisted that her grandchildren be quiet in church, and she taught them how to act around whites without losing their dignity. She did not hesitate to use the switch if they cursed or if their feet were not clean enough when they went to bed.

Of all the people in Maya's world, however, she loved her brother, Bailey Johnson, the most. A year older than Maya, Bailey was her best friend. He gave Marguerite her nickname, calling her "Mya Sister" soon after she was born. He then shortened it to "My" and later stretched it back to "Maya."

Angelou described what she and Bailey had done together. Their evening chores included throwing scoops of corn to the chickens and mixing dry sour mash, leftover food, and oily dishwater for the hogs. They played pop the whip, memorized their multiplication tables, and recited poetry to each other. They even went to the well at night, washing and then greasing their legs with cold Vaseline.

Angelou made sure her readers knew that Bailey was her hero. He could pray out loud in church and steal pickles out of the barrel while Uncle Willie stood nearby. He thought of the most daring routes when they played follow the leader. He was also better looking than she was. She wrote, "Where I was big, elbowy and grating, he was small, graceful, and smooth. … His hair fell down in black curls, and my head was covered with black steel wool."

Even years after she had grown up, Angelou remembered the hurt that Bailey and Maya felt at being sent to Arkansas, away from their parents. But when Maya next saw her mother, Vivian Baxter Johnson, waiting for her in St. Louis, she knew why they had been sent away. "She was too beautiful to have children," Angelou said. Besides her "fresh-butter see-through clean color," straightened hair, and red lipstick, Vivian laughed, told jokes, and had fun all the time. She even woke Maya and Bailey at 2:30 A.M. for a party with brown biscuits and hot chocolate she had made just for them.

CITY LIFE

Angelou's memories of her mother's life in "the Negro section of St. Louis" described an alternative way—besides farming and picking cotton—that blacks lived in the 1930s. Though gambling and drinking were against the law, people like Hard-Hitting Jimmy, Two Gun, and Poker Pete could be seen on the streets doing both. Maya and Bailey watched their mother sing and dance at a tavern. There, they learned the Time Step, a basic step to many dances. Vivian's mother controlled the neighborhood because she was politically important as a precinct captain, and she had six sons who enjoyed a good head-bustin', knuckle-splittin' fight when it was needed.

Angelou included in her book many details to show that city life was different from life in Stamps. She wrote how people ate thin-sliced ham, unlike Momma's half-inch slabs. Instead of just serving as a garnish under potato salad, lettuce was part of a sandwich. In St. Louis, people were not very polite, answering curtly, "Yes" or "No" rather than "Yes, ma'am," or "No, ma'am." Maya's school was even bigger than the white school in Stamps. Teachers, wrote Angelou, "walked with their knees together and talked through tight lips as if they were as afraid to let the sound out as they were to inhale the dirty air that the listener gave off." For seven-year-old Maya, St. Louis was just too much, and she retreated into the world of books whenever she could.

Six years later, 13-year-old Maya and 14-year-old Bailey again moved in with their mother, who had settled in California. Angelou carefully recorded life in San Francisco as blacks displaced the Asian population to work in shipyards and ammunition factories during World War II. She wrote, "Where the odors of tempura, raw fish and *cha* had dominated, the aroma of chitlings, greens and ham hocks now prevailed."

She told readers about her civics teacher, Miss Kirwin, who was the first white person to treat her without prejudice. She described Daddy Clidell, her mother's new husband, who acted more like a father than her biological father. Clidell wore a large, yellow diamond stickpin. He liked having Maya with him. He taught her to play poker and blackjack, and introduced her to the local con men: Cool Clyde, Tight Coat, and Red Leg.

Paul Laurence Dunbar (1872–1906) was the first African-American poet to gain national recognition. Maya Angelou took the title of her first autobiography, *I Know Why the Caged Bird Sings*, from a line in Dunbar's poem "Sympathy."

Angelou took the title of her autobiography *I Know Why the Caged Bird Sings* from a line in Paul Laurence Dunbar's poem, "Sympathy." (Dunbar, a son of former slaves who was born in 1872, was the first nationally recognized African-American poet. He was most famous for capturing the speech patterns of the black community in his writing. Maya Angelou read many of his poems when she was young.) In her book, young Maya is the "caged bird" because of her little-girl longings and because of the prejudiced attitudes she lived under.

She described herself as a "too-big Negro girl, with nappy black hair, broad feet and a space between her teeth that would hold a number-two pencil." Angelou admitted to her suspicion that she was an orphan picked up to keep Bailey company and that she dreamed of waking up as a white girl.

Maya was a captive to the memory of being raped by one of her mother's boyfriends. For five years, she did not talk to anyone but Bailey. The speaker at her eighth-grade graduation tried to imprison Maya in a bigot's view of her future. He told her and her classmates that they could hope to be athletes, but not doctors or scientists. She was hemmed in by her longing to fit in someplace.

"It was different than anything I'd ever read," said Loomis when Angelou sent her manuscript to him. "It was special and unique."

A BESTSELLER

Published in 1970, *I Know Why the Caged Bird Sings* was an immediate success. Angelou was the first African-American woman whose book was on the *New York Times* nonfiction bestseller list. The book was also nominated for a National Book Award.

James Baldwin, an African-American writer, called the book "a beginning of a new era in the minds and hearts of all black men and women." Critics were amazed at Angelou's "inner truthfulness." One reviewer said her book's beauty "is not in the story but the telling." Another said, "Maya Angelou writes like a song and the truth."

Angelou's word pictures were like images on a movie screen. She worked very hard to create them. She later said, "I try to pull the language into such a sharpness that it jumps off the page." Readers could imagine her father's voice when Angelou wrote that it "rang like a metal dipper hitting a bucket." They understood Uncle Willie's handicap when she said that he "sat like a giant Z" as he helped them with their homework. Her mother was "like a pretty kite that floated just above my head." Dolores, her father's girlfriend, "kept the house clean with the orderliness of a coffin." When Angelou wanted to show how Bailey struggled to keep quiet in church, she wrote, "Bailey's laugh had worked its way up through his body and was escaping through his nose in short hoarse snorts."

To explain the complete segregation she lived under in Arkansas, Angelou wrote, "People in Stamps used to say that the whites in our town were so prejudiced that a Negro couldn't buy vanilla ice cream. Except on July Fourth. Other days he had to be satisfied with chocolate."

Angelou also included funny stories in her book. During church service, an emotional Sister Monroe hit Reverend Thomas with her purse while he was preaching. "Before he could bring his lips together, his teeth fell, no actually his teeth jumped, out of his mouth," Angelou wrote. "The grinning uppers and lowers lay by my right shoe ..." Critics, reviewers, and readers all agreed that Angelou had written an autobiography as literature. Since then, scholars have studied every chapter, every paragraph, and every sentence in *I Know Why the Caged Bird Sings* from hundreds of different points of view. Article after article and shelves of books explain the themes, motifs, messages, and symbols that experts have found in

IN HER OWN WORDS...

The idea that you should never let life get you down is one that Maya Angelou tries to impart. She has said:

One of the first things that a young person must internalize, deep down in the blood and bones, is the understanding that although he may encounter many defeats, he must not be defeated.

Maya Angelou, in a 1971 photograph, holds a copy of her autobiography. *I Know Why the Caged Bird Sings* became an immediate success after its release the year before, and it remained on the bestseller list for three years. Her autobiography was also nominated for a National Book Award.

Angelou's book. They discuss everything from the role of the mother figure in black society to the importance of the fried chicken dinner in Angelou's work.

A STORY FOR EVERYONE

Some have called *I Know Why the Caged Bird Sings* a "coming of age" story about Maya's journey from childhood to adulthood. Others point to the progress she made from feeling unloved and unattractive to accepting herself. Those interpretations appeal to people of all races and ages who struggle with self-esteem.

Literary experts refer to the many terrible incidents in which the white world surrounded Maya's black world. They believe Angelou was writing about racial problems in America's troubled society.

Angelou, on the other hand, said she was writing about all people of all races. "I speak to the black experience, but I am always talking about the human condition—about what we can endure, dream, fail at and still survive."

The most important part in the title of Angelou's autobiography is not *caged bird* but the word *sings*. She showed that Maya did not blame anyone else for her experiences or become bitter from them—however difficult or horrible they might have been. Maya got through them to sing her own song of life.

Angelou has said, "All my work, my life, everything is about survival. All my work is meant to say, 'You may encounter many defeats, but you must not be defeated.'"

Angelou never intended to write any more of her life. She said, "I thought I was going to write *Caged Bird* and that would be it, and I would go back to playwriting and writing scripts for television."

Instead, *I Know Why the Caged Bird Sings* stayed on the best-seller list for nearly three years and sold several million copies. Vocabulary lists, lesson plans for teachers, study guides, and reading group guides for students are among nearly a half-million Websites mentioning the book. Over the next three decades, she would write five more autobiographies and many poems describing her thoughts and feelings. Not bad for a woman who could not resist a double dog dare.

2

Marguerite Ann Johnson: The Other Side of the Tracks

Today, three-year-olds can barely get through their ABCs. They take an afternoon nap, and watch Big Bird and Elmo on television. They need someone else to cut their meat and butter their bread.

But in 1931, three-year-old Marguerite Johnson (Maya) and her four-year-old brother, Bailey, were put on a train all by themselves. They traveled halfway across the country, from Long Beach, California, to Stamps, Arkansas, by themselves. They were sent like Federal Express packages. Instead of an address or postage, they wore tags on their wrists saying, "To Whom It May Concern—that we were Marguerite and Bailey Johnson Jr., going to Stamps, Arkansas, c/o Mrs. Annie Henderson."

THE SEGREGATED SOUTH

Stamps squatted in the Deep South. It was a hot, dusty town, held together by a lumberyard and cotton fields and split down the middle by racial prejudice.

"In Stamps, the segregation was so complete that most Black children didn't really, absolutely know what whites looked like," Angelou wrote in *I Know Why the Caged Bird Sings.* "Other than they were different.... I remember never believing that whites were really real ... their skin was too white and see-throughy, and they didn't walk on the balls of their feet the way people did—they walked on their heels like horses. People were those who lived on my side of town."

Old ideas stick in the mind. Years later, when Angelou visited Stamps as an adult, she could not bring herself to walk into the white part of town.

Jim Crow Laws

After the Civil War and Reconstruction, many Southern states passed Jim Crow laws. (The name "Jim Crow" is a reference to the minstrel character Jump Jim Crow, a racist depiction of a poor rural black man.) The laws were meant to separate the races in public places like schools, parks, hotels, trains, and buses. Signs saying "Whites Only" and "Colored" were posted at water fountains, restrooms, waiting rooms, and entrances to libraries, theaters, and courthouses. Mobs, like the Ku Klux Klan, went hand-in-hand with such humiliating laws. From 1880 to 1930, more than 3,700 men and women, mostly Southern blacks, were lynched.

Jim Crow laws also barred blacks from voting. Southern states required blacks, but not whites, to pay poll taxes and pass literacy tests. One literacy test involved reciting the entire U.S. Constitution by memory.

In 1896, the Supreme Court ruled that segregation was constitutional if different facilities for blacks and whites were of equal quality. This began "separate but equal" segregation. In the 1950s, civil rights groups worked to change the policy in trains and buses. Southern states complied with the new laws by allowing blacks on the same buses as whites but required them to sit in the back or give up their seats to whites. In 1964, federal civil rights legislation made discrimination illegal in public places, required employers to provide equal opportunities to all races, and made it possible for federal funds to be withdrawn from projects that discriminated on the basis of color, race, or national origin.

A separate drinking fountain for black people is seen on the county courthouse lawn in Halifax, North Carolina, in this 1938 photograph. Across the South, Jim Crow laws set up separate public facilities for blacks and whites. Stamps, Arkansas, where Maya Angelou lived with her grandmother in the 1930s, was no different.

The children's father had sent them to live with his mother, Annie Henderson, after he and their mother, Vivian Baxter, ended their marriage. Angelou later said of her grandmother, "I thought maybe she was God, with her mental repose, her serenity, her deep voice and great love."

Annie built the Wm. Johnson General Merchandise Store an equal distance between the lumberyard and the cotton gin, the two businesses that employed the most people in town. Years before the store became the discount super center of the 1930s, she divided her time between the two businesses. At lunchtime, she sat outside the workers' door of each, selling hot fried ham and chicken pies out of a coal pot. Workers liked her cooking and her fairness, and she made enough money to support her two small children.

The store was Maya's favorite place. She later wrote, "Alone and empty in the mornings, it looked like an unopened present from a stranger. Opening the front doors was pulling the ribbon off the unexpected gift." Inside, Maya waited on customers who bought corn for their chickens and food for themselves in five-cent sales.

Uncle Willie was the other important adult in her life. Younger than Marguerite and Bailey's father, he had been crippled as a baby. His face sagged down, his left hand was as small as a child's, and he walked with a cane. Marguerite loved him and once pretended to be his daughter when he talked to visitors from Little Rock. "Not only did I not feel any loyalty to my own father, I figured that if I had been Uncle Willie's child I would have received much better treatment."

Momma and Uncle Willie were loving, but strict, guardians. Nightly, Maya and Bailey had to go to the well, wash in ice-cold water, and then grease their legs with cold, stiff Vaseline. Momma would direct them to "wash as far as possible, then wash possible."

By the time Maya was five years old, she and Bailey knew their multiplication tables and completed their evening chores daily. Every Sunday, they sat through six hours of services at the Christian Methodist Episcopal Church.

Maya adored her older brother. He was her confidant, her protector, her avenger, and her advisor. Maya thought he could

IN HER OWN WORDS...

As a young girl, Maya Angelou immersed herself in the works of writers like Edgar Allan Poe and William Shakespeare. She said:

I already had an affection for Poe because I liked his rhythm. When I read Shakespeare and heard that music I could not believe that a white man could write so musically.

do anything: steal pickles right under Uncle Willie's nose, read more books than she did, and think up the best plans for all their games.

As a youngster, Maya fell in love with William Shakespeare. "He was my first white love," she wrote. "Although I enjoyed and respected Kipling, Poe, Butler, Thackeray, and Henley, I saved my young and loyal passion for Paul Laurence Dunbar, Langston Hughes, James Weldon Johnson, and W.E.B. Du Bois.... I pacified myself about his [Shakespeare's] whiteness by saying that after all he had been dead so long it couldn't matter to anyone any more."

Maya learned early on about the hate that whites felt toward those on her side of the tracks. She watched some children insult her majestic grandmother, an adult, outside the store just because she was black. Maya did not realize that, when Momma refused to sink to their level and return their insults, she triumphed over her tormentors.

REUNITED WITH HER MOTHER

When Maya was seven years old, her father reappeared to take her and Bailey back to their mother in St. Louis. Maya was shocked. Her parents were strangers to her. In her child's mind, she believed her parents were dead. She thought that was the only possible reason her parents would have abandoned her and Bailey. Then she believed that her father was the only "brown skinned white man" in the world and that her mother had given her away because she was too beautiful to have children.

Maya was born in St. Louis on April 4, 1928. But, of course, she did not remember anything about the hot, soot-covered town. When her father dropped them off, she and Bailey were thrown into yet another alien world. The best thing she could find in the city was a bag of jelly beans mixed with peanuts. In Stamps, peanuts were roasted in the oven at night. In St. Louis, the children attended Toussaint L'Ouverture Grammar School.

Because of their work in the store, Maya and Bailey were ahead of the other students in arithmetic and reading, so they were moved up a grade.

Vivian Baxter's "fresh butter color, white teeth and red lips" made Maya think that her mother looked just like the Virgin Mary. Her mother cut and straightened her hair, and Maya felt ugly next to her—to no one's surprise.

Vivian's brother, Maya's Uncle Tommy, told her, "Don't worry 'cause you ain't pretty. Plenty pretty women I seen digging ditches or worse. You smart. I swear to God, I rather you have a good mind than a cute behind."

Her other relatives were a tough lot. Her mother's mother, Grandmother Baxter, was a powerful political person in the city's black section. Grandfather Baxter told their mean, short-tempered sons, "If you're arrested for fighting, I'll sell the house, lock, stock and barrel, to get you out."

Eventually, the children moved from their grandparents' house to live with their mother and her boyfriend, Mr. Freeman. He changed her life. Later, Angelou would say that she has thought about what he did to her every day of her life.

One day, when her mother was away, Mr. Freeman raped Maya and threatened to kill Bailey if she told anyone. He sent her to the library, a walk of a thousand agonies. When she got home, she went to bed. Her mother thought she was getting sick until she discovered Maya's blood-soaked panties. Maya was hospitalized, and Mr. Freeman was arrested.

At the trial, eight-year-old Maya lied on the stand about a previous time he had molested her. Freeman was convicted, but before he served any time, he was killed. Authorities suspected he had been kicked to death. Grandmother Baxter hardly seemed surprised when she heard the news.

KEEPING SILENT

Maya thought that her testimony, and the evilness she believed her words held, cost Mr. Freeman his life. The third grader

Actress Diahann Carroll tries to console young Constance Good in a scene from the 1979 television movie *I Know Why the Caged Bird Sings*. Good played Maya as a child while Carroll portrayed her mother, Vivian Baxter. When Maya was eight years old, she was raped by her mother's boyfriend. Soon after, she stopped talking for several years.

decided, "If I talked to anyone else, that person might die too. Just my breath, carrying my words out, might poison people and they'd curl up and die like the black fat slugs that only pretended. I had to stop talking."

Maya's relatives in St. Louis were tolerant, at first, and then impatient with her silence. After whippings did not persuade her to talk, they sent both children back to Arkansas. Her grandmother Henderson told her, "Sister, Momma don't care. Momma know, Sister, when you and the good Lord get ready, you're gonna be a preacher." Maya's silence was accepted as the behavior of a "tender-hearted" child. Back in Stamps, where Maya believed whites were "like ghosts, that if you put your hand on your finger would go all the way through," the black community accepted her as the "Southern silent child." For five years, she spoke only to Bailey and wrote on a tablet to communicate with others.

She started writing around the age of nine, during her silent period. "It was my way of keeping in touch, I guess," Angelou said years later. "And I loved poetry.... I just loved it. I must have been the most tiresome kind of child—you know, not talking and weeping over poetry, which I half understood at that."

Then Maya met Bertha Flowers, a refined woman who wore voile dresses, a hat, and gloves. She invited Maya to her house for cookies and lemonade that she made especially for her. She encouraged Maya to talk. "Words mean more than what is set down on paper," she said. "It takes a human voice to infuse them with the shades of deeper meaning."

Mrs. Flowers lent Maya her books on the condition that she always read them aloud. She told Maya to come back with a poem ready to recite. She took her to the Stamps library and told her to read every book in the place.

"I didn't understand them all, but I read them anyway," Angelou later said, "I thought I was being singled out. You can't imagine how excited I was when I saw her come down the road with a big bag of books in her hand. I knew they were for me. So I read everything: I still do."

Mrs. Flowers's attention brought Maya's silence to an end. She realized that another person liked her for just being who she was.

GRADUATION DISAPPOINTMENT

It was never more clear that Maya lived on the other side of the tracks than during her eighth-grade graduation ceremony in 1940. In the first place, Lafayette County Training School was different from the white school. It lacked a lawn, a fence, and tennis courts. It sat on a dirt hill, and its playground was just rusty hoops on swaying poles. Still, graduating from eighth grade was an accomplishment that qualified some African Americans to become teachers in black schools.

Maya graduated near the top of her class. For the occasion, Momma had made her a buttercup yellow dress with intricate smocking, embroidered daisies, and crocheted lace on the collar. She oiled Maya's legs and tamed her wild hair into a braid. She even closed the store for the ceremony.

But a white politician, the graduation speaker, sullied the day with his prejudice. He told them about the microscopes and chemistry equipment coming to the white school. He pointed out that black children could try to succeed in athletics, but that they really had no future anywhere else.

Maya was infuriated that some white official had decided that only Jesse Owens and Joe Louis could be their heroes and that only white children could dream of being scientists or other professionals. "It was awful to be Negro and have no control over my life," she thought. "It was brutal to be young and already trained to sit quietly and listen to charges brought against my color with no chance of defense."

She did not hear her name called or her honors listed. Her special day was ruined. Then the valedictorian led the audience in singing the Negro National Anthem. Though she had sung the anthem since she was a toddler, she understood the words for the first time:

> We have come over a way that with tears has been
>   watered,
> We have come, treading our path through the blood of
>   the slaughtered.

The song made her realize that she was "a proud member of the wonderful, beautiful Negro race."

On the other side of the tracks, however, whites did not admire the "wonderful, beautiful Negro race." Maya was again reminded of that fact by a white dentist in Stamps. She had a toothache, and Momma tried to get him to ease Maya's pain. He refused to treat her toothache, even though he had once borrowed money from Momma to save his business. He told her that he would "rather stick my hand in a dog's mouth" than in a black person's. Momma insisted he pay her the interest on his loan—the price of two tickets to Texarkana to see a black dentist.

Bailey, too, met prejudice face to face. He was forced by white men to carry the bloated, mutilated body of a black man back to the jail. Because hate had come too close to those she loved, Momma soon sent Bailey and Maya to California, where their mother had moved.

OFF TO SAN FRANCISCO

In 1941, 13-year-old Maya left Stamps for San Francisco. As World War II began, she lived with her mother in their 14-room boarding house. She attended George Washington High School, and was one of the school's three black students. She was surprised by her civics and current events teacher, a white woman who treated all of her students with equal respect.

"Miss Kirwin never seemed to notice that I was Black and therefore different," Angelou wrote. "I was Miss Johnson and if I had the answer to a question she posed I was never given any more than the word 'Correct,' which was what she said to every other student with the correct answer."

At 14, Maya was self-conscious about her "cumbersome shaped body with its knobs for knees, knobs for elbows, and alas, knobs for breasts." Still, she received a scholarship to the California Labor School, where she took dance and drama classes at night.

Her mother, Vivian, married Daddy Clidell, who became as close to a father as Maya ever had. He owned apartment buildings and pool halls. He was a simple, honorable man. Maya looked enough like him for others to call her his daughter.

Her real father did not completely ignore her. He invited her to spend the summer with him in Southern California. His girlfriend, Dolores, did not like Maya. When she and her father returned from a trip to Mexico, Dolores started an argument, calling Vivian a whore. Maya slapped her. In the fight that followed, Dolores stabbed Maya in the back.

Maya ran away when she realized that her father had chosen Dolores's side over hers. For a month, she lived in a junkyard with a small group of runaways. Everyone worked at some job—collecting bottles, mowing lawns, or entering dance contests. They gave their money to Bootsie, the commune's leader. Maya learned a valuable lesson there.

"Odd that the homeless children, the silt of war frenzy, could initiate me into the brotherhood of man.... The lack of criticism evidenced by our ad hoc community influenced me, and set a tone of tolerance for my life."

A FIRST

At 15, Maya wanted to get a job instead of attending school. She had never taken typing or shorthand writing classes, so office jobs were out. She was too young to work in the war plants or shipyards. Though being a streetcar conductor for the Market Street Railway Company was off limits to black people, Maya was determined to wear the blue uniform of a conductorette. She waited three weeks for the white receptionist to give her an application form. She wrote that she was 19 (instead of her real age). She said she was the former companion and driver for Mrs. Annie Henderson in Stamps, Arkansas. Finally, she was hired. She was given early shifts, so she had to get up at 4:30 A.M., but she became the first black streetcar conductor in San Francisco.

Maya worried about her sexuality. She was tall, thin, flat-chested, and had a deep voice and big feet. She suspected that she was a lesbian. To find out if she was, she asked a popular neighborhood boy to have sex with her. The experience, without romance or emotions, changed her life. Three weeks later, Maya discovered she was pregnant. She hid her condition for more than eight months. Incredibly, her mother did not notice as Maya filled out. By the time the pregnancy advanced, Vivian had gone to Alaska to open a nightclub. After graduating from Mission High School, Maya wrote her family a note: "Dear Parents, I am sorry to bring this disgrace on the family, but I am pregnant. Marguerite."

Her family accepted her choice not to marry the father. "Well, that's that. No use ruining three lives," her mother said. Vivian, a registered nurse, helped deliver Clyde Bailey Johnson in July 1945. Maya's family embraced him as their own.

3

Rita Johnson: Mother and Wage Earner

Maya Angelou wrote down what happened during the next three years of her life in a second autobiographical volume, *Gather Together in My Name.* Maya bounced around the underside of society, trying to find a job to support her son and someone to belong to. At 17, she was enough of a little girl to dream about what a perfect life would be and enough of an adult to take care of Clyde.

Maya had taken responsibility for becoming pregnant. She said in *I Know Why the Caged Bird Sings,* "I hefted the burden of pregnancy at sixteen onto my own shoulders where it belonged." She made no excuses and blamed no one but herself. She did not do anything different after Clyde was born.

She never considered giving Clyde up for adoption or accepting government assistance. She did not even accept her mother's offer to care for Clyde. Maya did not want to leave her two-month-old baby with Vivian. After all, Vivian had not taken care of her own daughter. Maya felt guilty about living with her mother and stepfather. World War II was over, and many of the renters who stayed in Vivian Baxter's boarding-house were leaving.

Maya decided to get a job, leave her mother's house, and support her son by herself. Later, Angelou looked back on her decision: "I had no understanding about anything—I mean, utterly, so stupid that my face burns to think of it now. But I had the determination to raise my child."

Unfortunately, Maya had not learned any work skills in high school. Her job choices were limited. Blacks and whites had worked together during World War II, but racial preju-dice returned when the war ended. Her choices were nar-rowed further. She applied to be a telephone operator, but the company official told her she had "failed" a test. Supposedly, she had not been able to unjumble nonsense words into "cat," "rat," and "sat."

"We simply cannot risk employing anyone who made the marks you made," said the woman. Angelou described her as having "coifed hair, manicured nails, dresser-drawers of scented angora sweaters and years of white ignorance." The woman suggested there was an opening for a bus girl in the cafeteria.

CREOLE COOKING

Maya found another job. She saw a cardboard sign, "COOK WANTED. SEVENTY-FIVE DOLLARS A WEEK." She decided she could do anything for $75. "I knew I could cook Creole, whatever that was," she said.

She gave her name as Rita Johnson, thinking that Mar-guerite and Maya did not sound Creole. Reet, as her Creole Cafe employer nicknamed her, moved out of her mother's house into a room (with cooking privileges), bought furniture and a white chenille bedspread, and found a baby-sitter for Clyde. A boarder in her mother's house told her to just throw in onions, green peppers, and garlic, and she would be cooking Creole. "Surely, this was making it," Maya thought.

Working in the restaurant, Maya noticed Curly. "Butter-colored, honey-brown, lemon- and olive-skinned, chocolate and plum-blue, peaches and cream. Cream. Nutmeg. Cinnamon. I wondered why my people described our colors in terms of something good to eat," Angelou wrote in *Gather Together in My Name*. "Then God's prettiest man became a customer at my restaurant."

Curly had good table manners and smiled at Maya, but she did not think she had a chance with him. Her old insecurities flared up. "I never thought he would find me interesting, and if he did, it would be just to tease me," she later wrote.

When he learned that Maya was a single mother, he was sympathetic. His kindness touched her heart, and she quickly fell in love with the 31-year-old man. At last, she belonged to someone.

Or so she thought. They dated for two months. She bought him rings, a watch, and a sports coat. She took an interest in fashion and bought herself new clothes. It did not matter that he told her he would marry his real girlfriend in New Orleans when her job in San Diego ended. She pushed that fact out of her mind when they played with Clyde at the park or rode the Ferris wheel.

When Curly finally left, Maya was crushed. She moped around, rarely eating, losing weight, whining, and crying. She might have gone on like that indefinitely, but her brother, Bailey, who had been her strength in Stamps, would have none of her behavior. He told her, "Now, My, if you're happy being miserable, enjoy it, but don't ask me to feel sorry for you. If you want to stay around here looking like death eating a soda cracker, that's your business."

A CHANGE OF SCENERY

He gave her $200 to make a fresh start away from San Francisco. Her mother did not object. "You're a woman. You can make up your own mind," she told 18-year-old Maya. She gave

4520   U. S. NAVY PLANE CARRIER AT ANCHOR—LOOKING UP BROADWAY, SAN DIEGO, CALIFORNIA

A postcard from the 1940s shows a view of San Diego, California. For a short time in the late 1940s, Maya Angelou lived in San Diego. She worked as a waitress at the Hi-Hat Club, where sailors, prostitutes, and thieves gathered. Although she got caught up in the underside of life, she also found time in San Diego to discover the Russian writers Dostoevsky and Chekhov.

her a piece of advice. "Be the best of anything you get into. If you want to be a whore, it's your life. Be a damn good one. Don't chippy at anything. Anything worth having is worth working for."

Maya contacted her father's family in Los Angeles, hoping they might help her. She met with her aunts and uncles. They oohed and aahed over Clyde, but made it clear they expected them to leave. Maya and Bailey got on the train to San Diego, thinking they were the "meanest, coldest, craziest family in the world."

Maya found a job as a waitress in the Hi-Hat Club, where sailors, prostitutes, and thieves made contacts under the blaring music. Johnnie Mae and Beatrice, two lesbian prostitutes, befriended her at the club. Maya managed the money the two women earned. Dressed up in long skirts, Mexican off-the-shoulder blouses, sandals, and beads, she drove around in her new pale-green Chrysler convertible. She also spent her time in more appropriate ways. She discovered the Russian novelists Dostoevsky, Chekhov, and Maxim Gorki. Their world was just as gloomy and lonely as her own.

Maya's career as a madam lasted only two and a half months. In an argument about overnight customers, Johnnie Mae threatened to tell the police about Maya.

Angelou later wrote, "A numbing thought sidled across my brain like a poisonous snake. I might be declared an unfit mother, and my son would be made a ward of the court.... The tiny glands in my armpits opened and closed to the pricking of a thousand straight pins."

BACK IN STAMPS

She packed up Clyde, abandoned her green car at the train station, and headed back to her big, courageous, loving grandmother in Arkansas. She did not realize that Stamps had not changed. It was still divided by hate, and blacks were expected to know their place. Maya, however, had changed. She had experienced racial equality in San Francisco. Blacks could ride public transportation on a first-come/first-seated basis. More often than not, they were called Mr. or Mrs. at their jobs or by salesclerks.

Eight days after her arrival in Stamps, Maya crossed into "White Town" to go to the white general store. Dressed up San Francisco style, she walked the three miles in high heels, starched clothing, and gloves. In the store, a white salesclerk ordered her to move to the side in a narrow aisle and demanded, "How do you pronounce your name, gal? Speak up."

Maya had never been addressed as "gal" nor ordered by any white person to do anything. She drew herself up to her six-foot height and told the clerk: "If you have occasion to use my name, which I seriously doubt, I advise you to address me as Miss Johnson. If I have need to allude to your pitiful selves, I shall call you Miss Idiot, Miss Stupid, Miss Fool or whatever name a luckless fate has dumped upon you.... I'll slap you into the middle of next week if you even dare to open your mouth again."

News of the incident got back to Momma before Maya walked back home. Momma met her at the store's steps, and as Maya tried to explain herself, Momma repeatedly slapped her. "You think 'cause you've been to California these crazy people won't kill you? You think because of your all-fired principle some of the men won't feel like putting their white sheets on and riding over here to stir up trouble. Ain't nothing to protect you and us except the good Lord and some miles."

Momma quickly packed up Maya and Clyde and sent them back to San Francisco. Maya decided to join the U.S. Army for job training and money to buy a house. After passing the medical tests and signing a loyalty oath, she was set for induction. But the army discovered that she had attended the California Labor School. It was on the list of the House Un-American Activities Committee, suspected of being a Communist organization. The army rejected her.

A DANCING PARTNER

Her life took a dramatic turn after she landed a job as swing-shift waitress at the Chicken Shack. There, she met R.L. Poole. He was looking for a dance partner. Dancing was the one thing Maya had studied.

Her audition, in her mother's kitchen, was a joke. Sliding into the splits, her skirt ripped, her left foot got caught on a table, and the other one tangled with the gas heater. Trying to free herself, Maya pulled a pipe away from the stove. Gas escaped into the room until R.L. turned off the valve. He opened a window and moved the kitchen table so she could free her foot. She was humiliated. "My feelings were so hurt by the stupid clumsiness that I just rolled over on my stomach, beat my hands on the floor, and cried like a baby."

All R.L. could say was, "Well, anyway, you've got nice legs." He hired her, though, and took her to a rehearsal hall to learn the glides, taps, and slaps that would highlight his complex tap rhythms. "To be able to let my body swing free over the floor and the crushing failures of my past was freedom," Angelou wrote. "I thanked R.L. for my liberation and fell promptly in love with him."

Maya quit her job as a waitress. On stage, she loved the lights, music, tap rhythms, and the audience's applause. She rented a top hat, a cane, and a bathing suit-type costume with red, white, and blue sequins for her duets with R.L. She danced barefoot solos to "Blue Flame" and "Caravan," her ostrich feathers fluttering and Indian bells tinkling at her ankles. She believed that "Poole and Rita's dance team" would rocket into fame.

But then R.L.'s former girlfriend and dancing partner came to town. R.L. decided to replace Maya with her. Maya's world shattered. "All the doors had slammed shut, and I was locked into a too-tall body, with an unpretty face, and a mind that bounced around like a ping-pong ball," Angelou wrote. "I gave into sadness because I had no choice."

Instead of weeping and wilting, as she had done after Curly left her, 19-year-old Maya pulled herself together. "I had to find a job, get my grits together, and take care of my son," Angelou wrote. "So much for show biz, I was off to live real life."

Maya moved to Stockton, about 80 miles from San Francisco, to become a fry cook in a restaurant owned by a friend of her mother's. She found Big Mary, a neighborhood babysitter, to take care of Clyde during the week.

IN LOVE AGAIN

During her shift, Maya noticed L.D. Tolbrook. He was as old as her father, but he had a roll of money in his pocket and a diamond ring on his finger. He drove a silver-blue Lincoln. His official job was gambling, and he took Maya to neighboring towns to visit his business houses. Though he was married, he promised to leave his wife for Maya. His politeness and kindness impressed her. Once again, she fell in love.

He told her he had run up a $5,000 gambling debt. She volunteered to be a prostitute and give him the money. She might have fallen down the slippery slope to cocaine addiction, but she went back to San Francisco to be with her mother, who had had emergency surgery. There, Bailey found out about her prostitution career and opened her eyes to what she might become.

Maya returned to Stockton to get Clyde. But Big Mary had moved, taking Clyde with her. Maya frantically searched for them and finally found them in Bakersfield, 200 miles south. Reunited with three-year-old Clyde, she realized, "I had loved him and never considered that he was an entire person. He was three, and I was nineteen and never again would I think of him as a beautiful appendage of myself."

Back in the Bay Area, another man she met, Troubadour Martin, took Maya further into the dark, dangerous, slimy underworld. She was attracted to the tall, thin, handsome man. He told her, "Every time I used to see you, I thought to myself, 'That's a real nice lady.' Sure did." He asked if women could use her house to try on clothes, which he had probably stolen. Though he was heavily into drugs, Maya fell in love—again. She decided she would shoot up heroin if it would attract Troubadour to her.

One night she pressed him, crying and threatening to leave him unless he told her what he was into.

"Stop hiding what you do. I can take it," Maya told him.

But she could not.

Martin took her to a waterfront hotel. There, people sprawled on beds and sat on the floor in various stupors. Maya quickly realized she was someplace she should not be. "This was a hit joint for addicts. Fear flushed my face and neck and made the room tremble before me. I had been prepared to experiment with drugs, but I hadn't counted on this ugly exposure," she wrote later.

Troubadour, though, was not done with Maya's lesson. He took her into a bathroom and cooked heroin in a spoon.

"Shut up and watch this," he commanded. Before her horrified eyes, he bared his arm. Black scars and fresh, pussing sores covered it. He tied his arm tight with his tie, filled the syringe, and shot the heroin into his veins.

"You a nice lady.... I don't want to see you change," he said. "Promise me you'll stay like I found you. Nice."

She waited until the drug wore off, thinking about what she had seen. She later wrote:

> No one had ever cared for me so much. He had exposed himself to me to teach me a lesson and I learned it.... The life of the underworld was truly a rat race, and most of its inhabitants scurried like rodents in the sewers and gutters of the world. I had walked the precipice and seen it all; and at the critical moment, one man's generosity pushed me safely away from the edge.

The next day, Maya took Clyde and her belongings back to her mother's house in San Francisco. She was done with the dark, dangerous underbelly of life.

4

Maya Angelou: Dancer and Singer

Back in San Francisco, Maya rented a room and found two jobs, one in a real estate office and another in dress shop, to pay for a baby-sitter for Clyde. More important, she found a hiding place from her loneliness: the Melrose Record Store.

Its owner, Louise Cox, noticed Maya's frequent visits and asked her to be a salesclerk. Maya could not understand why Louise wanted to be friends. She was a white woman who wore perfume, cashmere sweaters, and pearls. Maya was black, tall, and skinny. Angelou later wrote in *Singin' and Swingin' and Gettin' Merry Like Christmas,* "My large extroverted teeth protruded in an excitement to be seen, and I, attempting to thwart their success, rarely smiled. Although I lathered Dixie Peach in my hair, the thick black mass crinkled and kinked and resisted the smothering pomade to burst free around my head like a cloud of angry bees.... I had to admit Louise Cox was not friendly to me because of my beauty."

Maya took the job. She dusted displays, emptied ashtrays, and waited on customers just as she had done at her grandmother's store in Stamps. She earned enough for Clyde, now five years old, to live with her full time. She moved back to her mother's house, appreciating more the woman who had told her to "row my own boat, paddle my own canoe, hoist my own sail..." and "if you want something done, do it yourself."

Still, Maya longed for a home and a man of her own. She later wrote:

> If I were married, "my husband" (the words sounded as unreal as "my bank account") would set me up in a fine house, which my good taste would develop into a home. My son and I could spend whole days together and then I could have two more children who would be named Deirdre and Craig, and I would grow roses and beautiful zinnias. I would wear too-large gardening gloves so that when I removed them, my hands would look dainty and my manicure fresh.

IN HER OWN WORDS...

Maya Angelou often mentions how a few words changed the way she thought about herself. Her mother, Vivian Baxter, was a beautiful woman who dressed in furs and diamonds. One day Baxter told her daughter that she was the greatest woman she had ever met. Angelou's reaction was:

> I got on the streetcar—I remember it so clearly, the time of day, the way the sun hit the seats—and I sat there and thought to myself, "Suppose she's right? Suppose I really am somebody? Suppose I really am a great woman?" I began to look at myself, to look at the things I was doing, the way I was living my life. I saw myself with these two jobs, raising a child, being independent and kind, and I thought, "Well, maybe I am!"

MARRIAGE

In 1950, she got her wish. Tosh Angelos was a Greek sailor whom Maya met at the record store. He was handsome and quiet. He liked Charlie Parker and other black jazz and blues musicians—unusual then for a white person. He and Clyde liked each other very much. She accepted when he proposed.

Maya's mother was not happy about Maya's marrying outside her race. "A white man? A poor white man? How can you even consider it?" she asked Maya.

Maya herself was not really sure why she was marrying him. The only reason she could give Vivian was "because he asked me, Mother."

Maya's dream, however, did not quite come true. Being married to Angelos came with a price. She was turned into a person quite different from the Maya who had taken care of her child by herself and had enjoyed reading books. Angelos made her quit her job. She became a "Good Housekeeping advertisement, cooking well-balanced, gourmet meals and molding fabulous Jello desserts. My floors were dangerous with daily applications of wax and our furniture slick with polish," Angelou wrote. Angelos also decreed that Clyde was too intelligent for his friends and made him give them up.

After two and a half years, Maya and Angelos realized they were not happy together and divorced. She was on her own once again, looking for a job.

SHE CAN DANCE

In 1953, she saw a sign outside a San Francisco nightclub advertising "Female dancers wanted. Good take-home pay." She auditioned for the job. After the owner of the Garden of Allah called for "the colored girl," Maya walked onstage without knowing what to do. She told the musicians, "I can dance, but I need something fast to dance to." She made up a dance, using every dance step she had ever learned. The drummer told her, "Baby, you didn't lie, you can dance."

Maya got the job. She liked dancing, six times a night, six days a week. But she did not like having to persuade customers to buy her a drink. She was paid a quarter for every drink and $2 for every bottle of champagne they bought. She decided she would not deceive the customers. She told them that her drinks were 7-Up instead of champagne, and they should decide if they wanted to buy her one, anyway. Men liked her honesty and sassy answers to their questions. Some even came back just to listen to her talk.

The job, however, lasted only three months. The other dancers who worked in the club were jealous that she made so much more money than they did. They told the boss that she was sleeping with the customers (which she was not), and she was fired.

It didn't matter. The manager, a couple of bartenders, and an entertainer from the Purple Onion saw her perform a few nights before her job at the Garden of Allah ended. They liked her dancing, and they had heard about her explanation of the drink scam. When they discovered she could sing calypso songs, they suggested she audition for the Purple Onion. They coached her on stage manners and suggested she make her name more exciting. They decided she should be Maya (Bailey's childhood nickname for her) Angelou (a variation of her married name, Angelos). They thought her image should be something other than a "tired old Southern Negro" and helped her invent a stage personality as a Cuban who could sing English but could not speak it. Maya added to the image, inventing a Watusi chieftain father and a "dark-eyed Spanish girl" for a mother.

Angelou left the fry-cook-bar-girl jobs forever. No more sweating over a stove. No more starched waitress aprons. At the Purple Onion, she danced barefoot, dressed in floor-length gowns. She was not a great singer, but the audiences loved her calypso songs. They loved her honesty. If she forgot some of the lyrics, she told the audience she would just dance. She became a star. She sang on television and was interviewed by

Maya Angelou began performing calypso songs at nightclubs in the 1950s. A stage persona was invented—she was a Cuban who could sing English but could not speak it. At this time, she also took the name Maya Angelou. Here, she appears in a promotional portrait taken for the cover of her 1957 album *Miss Calypso*.

newspaper and radio personalities. People recognized her on the street. She even had a 10-person fan club.

Everyone, it seemed, wanted her. A Broadway show, *New Faces of 1953*, wanted her to replace the famous singer Eartha Kitt. The Purple Onion wanted her to continue singing to large crowds at the nightclub. She added to her act by writing new calypso songs and composing melodies for poems she had written. An opera company wanted her as a dancer/singer in its production of *Porgy and Bess*.

She was invited to audition in New York for *House of Flowers*, a show starring the great Pearl Bailey. Standing onstage in front of the theater's velvet curtains, she tried to sing a song she did not know in a key she could not find. People backstage laughed, but Angelou, as always, would not give up. She decided to show the producers, who were watching from the darkened theater, exactly what she could do. She sang "Run Joe," a song from her act and danced her "special Saturday-night standing-room-only encore version. The one where I spun around, my body taut. The one where I yelped small noises and sighed like breaking ocean waves." Instead of laughter, Angelou heard enthusiastic applause when she finished. "You've got a certain quality," an official with the show told her.

Angelou's luck had indeed changed. On the same day, she received offers for a part in the *House of Flowers* production and the part of Ruby in the *Porgy and Bess* production, which was headed to Europe.

"There really was no contest," Angelou said about choosing *Porgy and Bess.* "I wanted to travel, to try to speak other languages, to see the cities I had read about all my life, but most important, I wanted to be with a large, friendly group of black people who sang so gloriously and lived with such passion."

AN INTERNATIONAL TOUR

In 1954, Angelou arranged for Clyde to stay with her mother and joined the production in Montreal, Canada. She was instantly welcomed by the 60-member cast. She began rehearsing her small part before they left for Italy. Learning her song was difficult for a singer who could not read music. Angelou had less trouble picking up the rhythms of her dance. She performed well on opening night in Italy. "You danced your tail off, girl," one friend said.

Angelou had stepped into another world. Buying a dictionary, she decided to teach herself Italian. "I would speak the language of every country we visited," she decided. "I would study nights and mornings until I spoke foreign languages." She was thrilled to see places she had read about in Shakespeare's works. Verona, where Romeo and Juliet had loved, was a long way from the dusty roads and stone-hard prejudice of Stamps, Arkansas. Inside the theaters, the Italians shouted "Bravo! Bravo!" for the cast of black Americans. On the streets, they treated the cast like heroes.

Paris, the company's next stop, greeted the cast even more enthusiastically. Originally scheduled for a three-week run, *Porgy and Bess* was held over for months. Staying in a hotel for

The cast of *Porgy and Bess* performed at the Theatre de l'Empire in Paris in September 1954. As part of the touring company, Maya Angelou visited Italy, France, Yugoslavia, Egypt, Morocco, and Spain. She made a point to learn the languages of the countries she visited and to get to know the local people.

so long cost too much. In order to send money home to Clyde, Angelou rented a small room, just big enough for a cot-sized bed and a suitcase. She shared the toilet down the hall with other boarders.

Cruising the nightlife in Paris, Angelou was recognized by the managers of two local nightclubs. They offered her jobs. Angelou's nights soon were divided into three performances: *Porgy and Bess*. a 12:30 show at the Mars Club, and a show at the Rose Rouge. She was a success in Paris. "The audience liked me because I was good enough," she wrote, "and I was different—not African, but nearly; not American, but nearly." People recognized her on the street. Some fans even sent her notes and flowers.

Angelou picked up another dictionary and studied Serbo-Croatian. The cast of *Porgy and Bess* moved on to Yugoslavia, the first American singers to go behind the Iron Curtain. The weather was gray and dreary. The company was told to stay together in the hotel and avoid wandering into the neighborhood.

Not Angelou. She had not studied Serbo-Croatian for nothing. She left the hotel in Zagreb. Her presence caused a near riot as people crowded in, trying to touch her. Walking into a music shop, Angelou asked for a mandolin. She was shocked when the woman clerk said, "Paul Robeson," the name of a famous black American singer and actor, and began singing "Deep River," a spiritual. Others in the store joined in with such feeling that Angelou was moved to tears.

She also strayed from a Belgrade hotel when a Yugoslav women invited her to go to a pre-Christmas party. "I divined that if I ever became rich and famous, Yugoslavia was not a country I would visit again," Angelou wrote. "Was I then to never see anything more than the selected monuments and to speak to no one other than the tour-guide spies who stuck so close to us that we could hardly breathe?"

At the party, Angelou was surprised to hear Billie Holiday, Sarah Vaughan, and Charlie Parker records. The party was

Porgy and Bess

Audiences in Europe and Africa loved the folk opera *Porgy and Bess*. George Gershwin wrote the music for the opera, and Ira Gershwin and DuBose Hayward wrote the text of the opera, based on Hayward's novel, *Porgy*. The opera was first performed in 1935.

The story takes place in the 1930s. Porgy, who lives in Catfish Row, South Carolina, is a crippled beggar who gets around in a goat cart. Bess is the girlfriend of a tough sailor, Crown. During a game of dice, Crown kills a man and escapes, leaving Bess behind. Just as the white police officers are about to capture her, Porgy hides Bess. Eventually, they fall in love. Crown later finds Bess at a church picnic and persuades her to leave with him, but Bess returns to Porgy after a few days. He still loves her and tells her he will protect her from Crown.

A hurricane strikes Catfish Row. One woman spies her man's overturned boat and rushes out into the storm. Only Crown will go with her. Townspeople fear that the fisherman, the woman, and Crown have died. But Crown returns. Just as he nears Porgy's hut to get Bess, Porgy stabs him. The police take Porgy away for questioning.

Sportin' Life, a drug dealer, gives Bess some cocaine and heroin. He tells her that Porgy will be found guilty and talks her into going to New York. Porgy gets out of jail, discovers that Bess is gone, and heads to New York on his goat cart to get her.

The opera attracted publicity from the beginning. Its story centered on a new subject, the black community, when some theaters were segregated and black opera singers were barred from singing at the Metropolitan Opera in New York. For many years, the black community criticized the opera, saying the story stereotyped blacks as poor and addicted to drugs. Protests began in the 1930s and continued through the civil rights movement in the 1960s and 1970s. Today, *Porgy and Bess* is recognized as one of the great cultural and operatic achievements ever written. "Summertime" is one of the most popular songs in the opera, and an estimated 2,500 versions have been recorded by many artists, including Billie Holiday, Frank Sinatra, Sam Cooke, and Janis Joplin.

going well until an old woman, the hostess's grandmother, entered the room. She saw Angelou and ran, squealing, back out the door. The hostess apologized, explaining that the old woman had never seen a black person before.

Angelou said, "I understand her. If I had lived that long and never seen a white person, the sight of one would give me a heart attack. I would be certain I was seeing a ghost."

When the old woman, dressed in a bathrobe and slippers, returned with her granddaughter, Angelou treated the old lady gently in spite of her insulting behavior. They spoke in Serbo-Croatian. The old woman patted Angelou's cheek when she left the room.

Porgy and Bess moved on to North Africa. The cast traveled on the famous Orient Express train and then boarded a boat for Alexandria, Egypt. Angelou was shocked by the cultural differences on the continent of her ancestors. In Alexandria, she noticed that many of the low-paying jobs were held by blacks, and the positions of authority were held by whites. Near the Great Pyramid and the Sphinx, she was nearly attacked by beggars who wanted her to give them money.

The company traveled on to Athens, Greece, and Tel Aviv, Israel, where Angelou taught ballet and African dance in exchange for lessons in Middle Eastern dance. The company next went to Morocco, Spain, and back again to France. The cast soon tired of being on the road.

WANTED AT HOME

Clyde thought the trip was too long, too. He wrote Angelou, asking, "When are you coming home, Mother? Or can I come and visit you." On one hand, Angelou missed Clyde. On the other, "dancing and singing every night with sixty people was more like a party than a chore."

Porgy and Bess moved on to Milan and was the first American opera to be presented at the famous La Scala opera house. It was another triumph for the troupe.

In Rome, the next destination, Angelou realized she was needed more at home than on stage. Her mother wrote to say she was going to Las Vegas to become a dealer in a black casino. There was no one to care for Clyde. He had also developed a mysterious rash that would not go away.

Leaving the company before the end of the tour had its price. Angelou had to pay her own way home as well as the expenses of her replacement. She needed $1,000 to do both. For two months, she performed with *Porgy and Bess*, sang at a nightclub, and taught dance classes to earn the money.

Back home, Angelou was surprised by her son. Nine-year-old Clyde had changed. His skin was flaked and scaly; his once wide smile had turned into shyness. He clung to Angelou, sitting in her lap, hugging her tightly, and finally asking her, in sobs, "When are you going away again?"

Angelou promised, "I swear to you, I'll never leave you again. If I go, when I go, you'll go with me or I won't go."

She blamed herself for leaving and causing such drastic changes in her son. She thought her guilt was driving her mad or worse yet, pushing her toward suicide. She went to the Langley Porter Psychiatric Clinic but decided the doctors could not help her. She fled to Uncle Wilkie, her old voice coach, pouring out her guilt and unhappiness to him. Finally, he told her to make a list of everything she should be thankful for. She wrote:

I can hear.

I can speak.

I have a son.

I have a mother.

I have a brother.

I can dance.

I can sing.

I can cook.

I can read.

I can write.

Suddenly she realized she had much more good in her life than bad. Uncle Wilkie told her, "Maya, you're a good mother. If you weren't, Clyde wouldn't have missed you so much.... Don't ask God to forgive you, for that's already done.... You've done nothing wrong. So forgive yourself."

Gradually things changed. Angelou's mood got better. Clyde no longer hovered close beside her or checked her bedroom to see if she was still there. His rash disappeared. He even changed his name, one day announcing he was no longer Clyde. Angelou had named him for the strong, sober Clyde River in Scotland, but she honored his wishes. Her son became known as Guy.

Angelou was offered a job singing in Hawaii. With Guy, she headed across the Pacific. Life was looking up.

5

The Activist

After working in Hawaiian nightclubs, Maya Angelou and Guy moved to Sausalito, California, and lived in a boat commune. She went barefoot, and wore jeans and unironed clothes. Looking back in *The Heart of a Woman*, Angelou recalled, "I allowed my own hair to grow into a wide unstraightened hedge, which made me look, at a distance, like a tall brown tree whose branches had been clipped."

Eventually, Angelou tired of their campout on the water. In 1958, they rented a place in Laurel Canyon, 15 minutes from famous—and primarily white—Hollywood. Billie Holiday, the legendary singer, visited her house, sang to Guy, ate a chicken dinner, and watched Angelou's nightclub act. Holiday told her, "You're going to be famous. But it won't be for singing." Neither woman realized how true that would be.

In 1959, Angelou began to write more song lyrics, some sketches, and short stories. She wrote and recorded six songs for Liberty Records. Writing, however, was not too important to Angelou until John Killens, an author who had come to Hollywood to write a screenplay of his book, read her work. The encounter set Angelou off in a new direction.

He told her, "You have undeniable talent. You ought to come to New York. You need to be in the Harlem Writers Guild." Angelou liked the idea. She needed a fresh start for herself and a change of scenery for 14-year-old Guy.

Settled in New York City, Angelou attended the Harlem Writers Guild, a group of African-American writers who met to critique one another's work. Like those who had joined before her, Angelou was required to read something she had written. The group gathered in a semicircle in John Killens's living room and took notes as Angelou read her one-act play, *One Love. One Life.*

Angelou was terrified. In *The Heart of a Woman*, she wrote, "The blood pounded in my ears but not enough to drown the skinny sound of my voice. My hands shook so that I had to lay the pages in my lap, but that was not a good solution due to the tricks my knees were playing. They lifted voluntarily, pulling my heels off the floor and then trembled like disturbed Jello."

After her reading, John Henrik Clarke remarked, "One Life. One Love? I found no life and very little love in the play from the opening of the act to its unfortunate end."

Humiliated and angered, Angelou would have run out of the house, but Killens urged her to show the group she could take the criticism. Then Clarke approached her as the group headed for refreshments. He said:

Maya, you've got a story to tell. We're glad to have you.... We remind each other that talent is not enough. You've got to work. Write each sentence over and over again, until it seems you've used every combination possible, then write it again. Publishers don't care much for white writers. You can imagine what they think about black ones.

John Killens, the author of *Youngblood*, invited Maya Angelou to join the Harlem Writers Guild after reading her work. She received some harsh criticism of her writing at her first meeting. Although stung, Angelou was determined to meet the challenge.

Before the party broke up, Paule Marshall, another writer, encouraged her to revise her play. She said, "You know, lots of people have more talent than you or I. Hard work makes the difference. Hard, hard unrelenting work."

Angelou had not decided to rewrite the play, but as she left the meeting, she asked Killens what he thought was the most difficult literary form. When he told her short stories, she said: "John, put me down for a reading in two months. I'll be reading a new short story. Good night."

Like Angelou would later do with her autobiography, she could not resist the challenge of doing the impossible. "I had to try," Angelou later wrote, "If I ended in defeat, at least I would be trying. Trying to overcome was black people's honorable tradition."

TOWARD ACTIVISM

The civil-rights movement was in full swing at that time. Many people were questioning society's traditions and laws. Blacks and whites protested the South's segregation laws, staging freedom marches and sit-ins. Angelou became unhappy with just singing cute songs in nightclubs. Her friends were speaking out against prejudice in their music, plays, books, and songs. Angelou wanted to contribute to the cause. She decided to quit show business.

Two weeks after she made her decision, she was invited to perform at the Apollo Theater in Harlem. She thought a show at the famous theater was a good way to end her singing career.

To end her act, Angelou wanted to perform an audience participation song. The Apollo's manager told her that the audiences would laugh her off the stage. Angelou dug in. "Thanks for your advice," she responded. "I'm going to sing it anyway."

Wearing a blue chiffon gown, matching heels, and a "natural" hairstyle, Angelou sang her calypso, blues, and Cuban songs. When she came back for her encore, she explained that "Uhuru" meant "freedom" in Swahili.

"If you believe you deserve freedom, if you really want it, if you believe it should be yours, you must sing," she told the audiences. And they did—for six days, three shows a day.

Angelou edged closer and closer to the civil-rights movement. She attended a fundraising rally for the Southern Christian Leadership Conference (SCLC) at a Harlem church. Hearing the Reverend Dr. Martin Luther King, Jr., inspired her and her friend Godfrey Cambridge to raise money for the cause.

With the SCLC's approval, they contacted actors from *Porgy and Bess*; located singers, dancers, and musicians; and looked for a theater. Angelou volunteered to write the script for the show. For once, her courage and determination failed her. No words worthy of the cause would come. She told Cambridge, "I can't write a play. I don't even know where to start.... I've agreed to do something I can't do."

Cambridge suggested that the entertainers perform acts they knew instead of learning an entirely new play. *Cabaret for Freedom* quickly became an evening of song, dance, comedy routines, and skits.

Angelou was back on track. Though she did not know how to run the mimeograph machine, type, or make a stencil, she volunteered to handle publicity. Her organizational skills were noticed by others, and she would soon take on another career. It would lead her directly into the center of the civil-rights movement.

In the meantime, *Cabaret for Freedom* closed, and she took a job that required a two-week stay in Chicago. When she returned, she discovered that a neighborhood gang had threatened Guy. Angelou would have none of that. She marched to a gang member's home and showed him a loaded gun, saying, "If the Savages so much as touch my son, I will then find your house and kill everything that moves, including the rats and cockroaches." Guy had no more trouble with the gang.

A NEW CAREER

In 1960, Angelou got a job offer she could not refuse. Members of the Southern Christian Leadership Conference wanted her to replace Bayard Rustin as the northern coordinator. They had watched how she handled *Cabaret*.

"We think you've got administrative talent," one member said. "We watched how you dealt with that cast," said another. "You kept order; and if anybody knows, I know the egos of actors. You never raised your voice, but when you did speak, everyone respected what you had to say."

Thirty-two-year-old Angelou became a full-fledged civil-rights worker. She organized fundraising meetings and dinners, wrote letters, asked for donations, and spoke for the cause.

Two months later, Angelou found Dr. King sitting in her office. He thanked her for her efforts and asked about her family. Reluctantly, she told him that Bailey was in prison for selling stolen goods. King was sympathetic. "Disappointment drives our young men to some desperate lengths. That's why we must fight and win," King said.

Harlem was brimming with activity. Protest marches were common. Black nationalists gave speeches, demanding freedom. Black Muslims campaigned for total segregation from white society. In September 1960, thousands poured into the streets to welcome Fidel Castro, the Cuban prime minister, and the entire Cuban delegation to a Harlem hotel. He stayed there, waiting to address the United Nations. A couple of days later, Angelou watched as Premier Nikita Khrushchev of the Soviet Union met the Cuban leader on the streets of Harlem.

For all of Angelou's involvement with the SCLC, she was a lonely woman. She met Thomas Allen, a bail bondsman. Though she liked his gentleness, kindness, and courtesy, he had no interest in her work in the civil-rights movement. His conversations were short sentences with words like "OK" and "no." Angelou did not love him, but she might have married him anyway. Then she heard Vusumzi Make (Mah-kay) talk.

A NEW LOVE

It was love at first sight. It did not matter to Angelou that the South African freedom fighter was fat and three inches shorter than she was. When he spoke of his struggle against injustice in his country, she promptly threw away Thomas Allen and their impending marriage.

Make was drawn to Angelou as well. He told her, "I intend to change your life. I am going to take you to Africa." Within a week, Angelou fell under his spell and told Make she would marry him.

Strong-willed, independent, high-spirited Angelou again became a meek housewife. She wrote later, "It seemed to me that I washed, scrubbed, mopped, dusted, and waxed thoroughly every other day. Make was particular. He checked on my progress. Sometimes he would pull the sofa away from the wall to see if possibly I had missed a layer of dust."

Make took control of her life. He made her quit her job at the SCLC. He gave her a household and food allowance, a little cash, but would not tell Angelou where he got his money. Used to being in charge, she was bothered by her new lifestyle. "I was as tight as a fist balled up in anger. My nerves were like soldiers on dress parade, sharp, erect, and at attention," she later wrote.

Angelou belonged to a group of women artists who supported the civil-rights movement. In January 1961, Patrice Lumumba, an African nationalist leader in the Congo, was assassinated. The women wanted to honor the fallen leader. They planned a small, silent tribute as the official announcement of the man's death was read at the United Nations. A half-dozen women intended to pin mourning veils over their faces, and a few men would wear elastic black armbands.

Word of their demonstration spread in Harlem. Thousands appeared at the United Nations, clogging the sidewalks and jamming the streets. They carried signs saying "FREEDOM NOW," "BACK TO AFRICA," "AFRICA FOR THE AFRICANS," and "ONE MAN, ONE VOTE."

About 75 protesters found seats in the General Assembly. They waited for the announcement of Lumumba's death. Suddenly, a protester screamed, and the carefully planned silent

African nationalists and other protesters demonstrated in 1961 in the General Assembly of the United Nations after the announcement of the assassination of Patrice Lumumba, a leader in the Congo. Maya Angelou was part of a group of women artists who had planned a silent tribute at the United Nations. After the announcement of Lumumba's death, a protester screamed, and the demonstration turned into a riot.

demonstration turned into a riot. Protesters yelled, "Murderers," "Baby killers," "Slave drivers." The guards shouted, "Get out. Get out." The United Nations delegates quickly emptied the Assembly. Angelou later wrote, "The balcony was ours. Just as in the Southern segregated movie houses, we were in the buzzards' roost again."

Outside, the crowd shouted at the police who gathered around them. Angelou and the other organizers moved the protesters away from the United Nations building. Newspaper and television reporters waded into the protesters, trying to get an interview.

"The day had proven that Harlem was in commotion and the rage was beyond the control of the NAACP, the SCLC, or the Urban League," Angelou later wrote.

Worried that the anger in Harlem would turn on itself, Angelou and her friend Rosa Guy asked Malcolm X if the Black Muslims could help keep order in the community. The famous spokesman for the Black Muslims condemned the demonstration. He said blacks should not protest in front of whites. Instead blacks should separate from them.

Later, he issued a statement that the women's riot was "symbolic of the anger in this country" and that black people were "letting white Americans know that the time is coming for ballots or bullets."

RETURN TO THE STAGE

Angelou considered returning to the theater. Her husband was busy traveling for the cause of freedom, and 15-year-old Guy was busy learning the ways of girls. Then, Angelou was offered a part in *The Blacks*, an off-Broadway play by Jean Genet. At first, she turned down the offer. She did not agree with the play's theme—that given the chance, blacks would become just as cruel as the whites who ruled them. Then she mentioned the offer to Make. He read the play and told her to take the part.

This was not the Maya Angelou of the UN protest. This Maya, meek and loyal, said nothing to contradict him. She joined her friend Godfrey Cambridge from *Cabaret for Freedom* and other well-known actors in the cast. Angelou was assigned the role of White Queen. Wearing a white mask, she used her role "to ridicule mean white women and brutal white men who had too often injured me and mine. Every inane posture and haughty attitude I had ever seen found its place in my White Queen."

The theater's bright lights became a shelter for Angelou. There was trouble at home. She found lipstick and makeup on her husband's clothes. They were not hers. He told her, "You are my wife. That is all you need to know." She received telephone calls from Make's political enemies, telling her that Make had been shot in Harlem or that Guy had been involved in a serious accident. Then, the sheriff's deputies arrived with an eviction notice. They were ordered to leave their apartment within 24 hours for not paying their rent.

Angelou and Guy were stunned. They had lived through tough times, sharing the same hotel room and eating food cooked on an electric burner, but they had never been kicked out of their home before. Make, however, was not worried. He told them, "I have a lot of money, so there's nothing to worry about." He found a hotel room. They lived there for three weeks while he made arrangements to move to Cairo, Egypt.

6

Maya Angelou Make: African

Maya Angelou and Guy left the United States, with its civil unrest, for a strange and exciting world. In Cairo, they saw camels, goats, mules, people, and limousines along the street. Vendors cooked on grills. Angelou could smell the food, spices, manure, flowers, and body sweat.

Make greeted Angelou and Guy at their apartment. He had decorated it with grand Oriental rugs, antique furniture, and tapestries. The sheets and towels were embroidered. A private doorman stood guard at the entrance, and a gardener tended their private garden.

Angelou met her husband's friends. Freedom fighters, diplomats, and ambassadors came to see Make's new wife. Guy went to American College, a school outside Cairo. He and his mother made a game of learning, competing to see who could learn the most Arabic vocabulary and speak with the best accent.

Make introduced her to David DuBois, an American journalist. Hearing him talk for the first time, Angelou felt a twang of homesickness. "The voice of an adult American black man has undeniable textures," she wrote in *The Heart of a Woman*. "I had forgotten how much I loved those sweet cadences."

At the many dinner parties Make told her to organize, DuBois and Angelou sometimes sang spirituals to reconnect with something American while they were so far from home.

IN NEED OF WORK

Angelou, Make, and Guy lived in grand style. They gave elaborate dinner parties. Guy's school was expensive. Once again, Angelou discovered that Make had not been making payments on the rugs, or the furniture, or the rent, or Guy's schooling. Creditors showed up at the door to take back their property. Desperate for money, she contacted DuBois.

"If I can get a job," she told him, "I'll handle the rest of it. I've been through too much to turn back now. I've been a fry cook, a waitress, a strip dancer, a fundraiser. I had a job once taking the paint off cars with my hands. And that's just part of it."

DuBois found her a job with an English-language magazine called the *Arab Observer*. The situation was awkward. She was a woman; she was not Egyptian, or Arabic, or Muslim. She was not much of a published writer. She had only written one short story for a Cuban magazine, songs for a couple of record albums, and some unpublished poems. Worst of all, she did not know anything about her new job as an associate editor.

Angelou did what she had always done. She found out what she needed to know. She went to the library and read all she could on Africa and journalism. She also read about editing and publishing. She studied newspapers, magazines, and essays. She listened carefully to coworkers. She asked her husband about the countries in Africa. She worked 10 hours a day. During the year she worked there, she gradually gained the respect of her colleagues, earned a raise from her boss, and received a few compliments from readers.

She added to her income by writing commentary for Radio Egypt, earning four pounds for a review (about $1.00 in today's money) and an additional pound for her narration.

MARITAL PROBLEMS

Angelou and Make's marriage was dying. He had not wanted her to work, even though he provided little money for expenses. He stayed away from home. He started seeing other women. Finally, he admitted to Angelou what he was doing. She later wrote, "I wanted to slap him until he snapped and split open like popcorn."

The pair appeared before an African palaver, a court of their friends who heard both spouses explain themselves before determining the couple's future. They took Angelou's side, but asked her to stay with Make for six more months. She agreed.

In 1962, when the six months had passed, Angelou and Guy left Make in Egypt. She got a job with the Liberian Department of Information and enrolled 17-year-old Guy in the University of Ghana. She intended to get him settled in his new school before going to Liberia. Three days into her two-week visit, however, her world turned upside down.

Guy was in an automobile accident. He had been hit by a truck. A friend told her, "He's in Korle Bu Hospital. But I swear, he's still breathing." He had a broken neck in three places, a broken arm, and a broken leg. Doctors covered his head, neck and shoulders, leg, and arm in what Angelou called a "prison of plaster."

Angelou would not leave him. She quit her Liberian job and found one at the University of Ghana as an administrative assistant. She rented a room at the YMCA. She cooked meals for Guy at a friend's house during his month-long stay at the hospital. She hitchhiked or took a taxi to see him every day.

After four months, Guy recovered enough to settle into his new school. Alone for the first time since she was 17, 33-year-old Maya Angelou Make did not feel as empty or as lonely as she thought she would. Angelou ended the fourth volume of her autobiography, *The Heart of a Woman,* by saying, "At last, I'll be able to eat the whole breast of a roast chicken by myself."

AT HOME IN GHANA

In Ghana, Angelou, the African American, thought she was "home." Feeling unwanted by white America, she settled in the land of her ancestors, Africa. Ghana was ruled by black Africans under laws made by black Africans and enforced by black Africans. It was hard, Angelou later admitted, to give up her American attitudes. She finally realized that, when she was rejected for a job, it was not because she was black. Everyone in Ghana was black. Ghana's president, Kwame Nkrumah, encouraged American blacks and African revolutionaries to come to his new, young country. In her fifth volume of autobiography, *All God's Children Need Traveling Shoes,* Angelou wrote: "For the first time, we could not lay any social unhappiness or personal failure at the door of color prejudice."

Angelou liked the Ghanaians who lived around her. "Their skins were the colors of my childhood cravings: peanut butter, licorice, chocolate, and caramel. Theirs was the laughter of home, quick and without artifice. The erect and graceful walk of the women reminded me of my Arkansas grandmother ..."

W.E.B. DuBois and his wife, Shirley Graham, led 200 black Americans who had settled in Ghana. They all noticed, and were a little puzzled, that the Ghanaians did not fawn over them for moving to their country. Though they were kind, Angelou noticed their distance. And after an assassination attempt on President Nkrumah, the black Americans were viewed with suspicion.

Sometimes, though, Angelou felt a part of Africa. She adopted the flowing fabrics and head wraps of the Ghanaian

President Kwame Nkrumah of Ghana (right) sits with Queen Elizabeth II of Great Britain and her husband, Prince Philip, during a ceremony in Accra, Ghana, in November 1961. Nkrumah encouraged black Americans to settle in his newly independent country.

women. She had her hair braided in the Ghanaian style. "My skin color, features, and the Ghana cloth I wore made me look like any young Ghanaian woman," she later wrote. "I could pass if I didn't talk too much."

She learned the Ghanaian traditional handshake–finger snap. She studied Fanti, Ghana's language, just as she had studied the languages of Italy, France, and Yugoslavia. "The music of the Fanti language was becoming singable to me," she wrote, "and its vocabulary was moving orderly into my brain."

Angelou was paid $200 a month for keeping records of student absences and requests for transfers, selling tickets for theater shows, filing, and typing. It was difficult to make ends meet, so she found a second job, writing commentaries on black American issues for the *Ghanaian Times.*

She settled into the life of Accra, Ghana's capital. She hired a "small boy" to do household chores. She attended a baby's "outdooring," an African tradition that invited family and friends to see the new arrival. Just as everyone else did during a harvest festival, she bounced up and down and waved a white handkerchief above her head as the royal chieftains passed. They were "black beyond ebony," clothed in gold and rich cloth, and were carried in hammocks before the thousands of spectators.

One weekend, Angelou drove her Fiat into the bush outside Accra. When she stopped in Dunkwa to rent a room for the night, she was thoroughly inspected. Dressed in her Ghana cloth and speaking Fanti, she was accepted by the townspeople as an African from Liberia. They welcomed her into their home as an honored guest. She sat in the yard, outside their thatched-roofed house while stew cooked over an open fire. To Angelou, the feeling was wonderful. "For the first time since my arrival, I was very nearly home. Not a Ghanaian, but at least accepted as an African."

CONNECTED TO AMERICA

Still, despite the kinship of color in Ghana, Angelou could never quite give up her American culture. She dated an attractive man from Mali, but she refused his proposal to be his second wife and move her family to Mali to live with him.

"As a Black American woman, I could not sit with easy hands and an impassive face and have my future planned," Angelou later wrote. "Life in my country had demanded that I act for myself or face terrible consequences."

Something as small as a package from the United States provided excuse enough for Angelou and her black American friends to meet. No one would admit to being homesick for the country they had left because of its prejudice and hate. But they loved reading American newspapers and devoured American food that friends and family sent.

Word reached the black Americans that Martin Luther King, Jr., was planning "The March for Jobs and Freedom" in Washington, D.C. They decided to support the march, scheduled for August 28, 1963, by organizing a similar demonstration in Ghana. They marched to the American Embassy to deliver a letter of protest to the American ambassador. A few carried sticks with oil rags for light as they walked and sang throughout the night. A thunderstorm drenched the marchers, who included Peace Corps volunteers and black Americans visiting Accra. Guy and other university students showed up. They had no way of knowing that the more than 200,000 demonstrators gathered at the Lincoln Memorial were listening to King deliver one of history's greatest speeches:

> I have a dream that one day this nation will rise up
> and live out the true meaning of its creed: "We hold
> these truths to be self-evident: that all men are cre-
> ated equal." I have a dream that one day on the red
> hills of Georgia the sons of former slaves and the
> sons of former slave owners will be able to sit down
> together at a table of brotherhood.

At dawn, two soldiers raised the flag over the U.S. Embassy in Ghana. The protesters shouted insults from across the street. But the truth could not be denied. Despite the wrongs done to black Americans in the United States, Angelou realized that she was not only African, she was an American as well. Having delivered the marchers' letter of protest, Angelou wrote, "I went home alone, emptied of passion and too exhausted to cry."

MEETING WITH MALCOLM X

Angelou again met Malcolm X in 1964, when he stopped in Ghana on his way back to the United States. He had gone to Mecca, the most holy city in Islam, and visited other African nations. His goal, he told Angelou and her friends, was to bring U.S. racism before the United Nations, much like South Africa's freedom fighters had done with apartheid. He urged Angelou and her other black American friends to come back to the United States. "The country needs you. Our people need you," he told her. "You have seen Africa, bring it home and teach our people about the homeland."

After Malcolm X's departure, Angelou looked carefully at her life. Although she enjoyed watching Ghanaian children

Malcolm X

Malcolm X was a controversial African-American activist during the 1950s and 1960s. While serving a 10-year jail sentence for burglary in the late 1940s, he became interested in the teachings of Elijah Muhammad, the leader of the Nation of Islam (or Black Muslims). Muhammad preached that white society was evil. He wanted African Americans to live separate from whites.

After Malcolm was paroled in 1952, he worked for Elijah Muhammad. He replaced his last name, Little, with an "X," like the brand that slave owners burned in the forearms of their new slaves. Malcolm X quickly made headlines, calling white people "devils" and talking about vengeance against them. Membership in the Nation of Islam grew from 500 to 30,000 over the next decade.

He left the Nation of Islam after learning of his leader's many affairs with women. Malcolm X formed the Muslim Mosque, Inc., and the Organization of Afro-American Unity (OAAU). Nation of Islam members hated Malcolm.

Malcolm X reversed his beliefs after taking a pilgrimage to Mecca, the holy city of Islam. There, he saw people of all races worshipping together. He wrote, "America needs to understand Islam, because this is the one religion that erases from its society the race problem." He said that not all whites were evil and that blacks might be able to work through existing avenues toward social justice.

His new ideas were not popular with black nationalists. On February 14, 1965, his house was firebombed. He, his wife, and his four children escaped unharmed. But on February 21, 1965, at an OAAU rally in Harlem, gunmen rushed the podium where Malcolm X was speaking. They shot him 15 times. At least two of the three men convicted in the killing had ties to the Nation of Islam. Malcolm X was 39 years old when he died.

Malcolm X (right) and the Reverend Dr. Martin Luther King, Jr., converse before a press conference in 1964. Malcolm X met with Maya Angelou that year in Ghana and urged her and other black Americans to return to the United States. "You have seen Africa, bring it home and teach our people about the homeland," Malcolm X told Angelou.

playing, and valued the forests and bush villages, she felt uneasy. "Ghana was beginning to tug at me and make me uncomfortable, like an ill-fitting coat," she said.

Closer to her heart, Guy was trying out his new manhood. Sporting a mustache, he had a girlfriend who was a year older than Angelou. "Oh Mother, really. Don't you think it's time I had a life of my own," he asked when Angelou objected. Rather than try to break the couple up and anger her son, she decided to leave Ghana. She took a job playing her old role as the White Queen when *The Blacks* toured Germany and Italy.

Back in Ghana, Angelou received a letter from Malcolm X with news of his new project, the Organization of Afro-American Unity (OAAU), news of his family, and news of the many death threats he received. He asked her to return to the

United States to be a coordinator for the OAAU. As she had done for Dr. King's SCLC, she would be raising money, writing news releases, typing, filing reports, and answering the phone—all for very little money. At first, she was undecided. Guy encouraged her, "Yes Mom," he told her, "It is time for you to go back home." He, however, wanted to stay in Ghana.

She decided to leave Africa, thinking she "had gotten all Africa had to give." Africa, however, was not quite finished with her.

Angelou had one more journey to make, straight into her past and Africa's heart. Her adventure began when a friend took her to see a small village about 30 miles from Accra. In Keta, Angelou climbed a narrow stairway, where she was stopped by a village woman. The woman spoke angrily to her, forcing her back down the steps. When Angelou could see her clearly, she was shocked. She was over six feet tall. Her lips, eyes, and cheekbones looked like those of Momma Henderson, Angelou's grandmother.

At first, the village woman did not believe Angelou was an American. When Angelou's companion convinced her, she became very sad. She led Angelou through the marketplace, stopping at stalls so other women could see her. They, too, became very sad, crying and groaning, as they looked at Angelou. They each gave her produce from their shelves—tomatoes, onions, peppers, yams, and cocoa yams.

Angelou learned that long ago Keta had been raided by slavers. A few children escaped into the woods. They watched "mothers and fathers take infants by their feet and bash their heads against tree trunks rather than see them sold into slavery." The adults were killed or kidnapped, and the village was burned.

The Keta women were descendants of the escapees and believed Angelou was a descendant of the captured adults. When Angelou heard the story, she joined the women in their tears. She cried both for the tragedy of lost people and for the last lesson Africa had to teach her. She later wrote, "Despite the murders, rapes and suicides, we had survived. The middle passage and the auction block had not erased us. Although separated from our languages, our families and customs, we dared to continue to live."

Angelou left for the United States, wearing her West African dress. She knew she was leaving the continent, but she also knew she was taking its spirit with her. She headed back to Malcolm X and his organization. Two days after she returned, on February 21, 1965, he was assassinated.

7

The Writer

Maya Angelou heard about Malcolm X's death in San Francisco. She had gone there to visit her mother and Bailey before starting to work for him. Shell-shocked by his death, she accepted Bailey's suggestion to go to Hawaii with him. There, she found work singing her calypso songs, but her heart had never been in singing. "I didn't care enough for my own singing to make other people appreciate it," she wrote in the sixth volume of her autobiography, *A Song Flung Up to Heaven.*

What she did care about was writing. She returned to Los Angeles, rented a one-room apartment, and landed a job with a research company. She hoped the job, asking consumers questions about cereal, dishwashing liquid, and peanuts, would not keep her from finishing a stage play she had started or from polishing poems she had written.

She was assigned to canvass Watts, a largely African-American area in southeast Los Angeles. While she walked door to door, she learned the mood of Watts. The area was like dry kindling, waiting for a match. Men were out of work; women labored to keep their families going. Children were left on their own, forming substitute families in gangs. Many dropped out of school. Goods were more expensive and of lesser quality than in the white neighborhoods.

On August 11, 1965, two white policemen stopped a car driven by an African American because it was swerving on the road. When the driver's mother arrived on the scene, a struggle erupted. The police arrested the driver, his brother, and their mother. Afterward, the crowd that had gathered went wild. Cars and trucks were overturned and burned. Stores were set on fire. Mobs grew into the thousands, roaming the streets and throwing bottles, rocks, and Molotov cocktails. Snipers shot at firefighters and ambulances when they came to help.

Angelou drove into Watts to see for herself what was happening. She saw looters carrying off radios, television sets, and clothing. She heard people screaming, burglar alarms blaring, and sirens wailing. Smoke gagged her. Policemen in gas masks grabbed people on the streets. Angelou ran.

Two days later, she returned to Watts, prepared to be arrested in the continuing riots. Her mother had once said, "Nothing's wrong with going to jail for something you believe in." This time she saw a car full of whites being rocked by young blacks. Policemen marched men in handcuffs right by Angelou, but they did not bother her. When the rioting finally ended, more than 35 people had died, 1,000 were injured, nearly 4,000 were arrested, and property damage totaled $100 million. The people of Watts had finally gotten the attention of the politicians.

Meanwhile, Angelou drifted back into the arts. She played a nurse in a production of *Medea* at the Theater of Being. She finished her play, *All Day Long*. But Angelou could not interest anyone in a "new play by an unknown playwright who also happened to be black and female." She wrote about a 13-year-old black boy whose move North introduced him to flush

The Watts Riots

On August 11, 1965, a routine traffic stop in Watts, in southeast Los Angeles, ignited seething frustration against racial discrimination. Until the National Guard brought about order, the burning, looting, and violence lasted six days. More than 35 people died, 1,000 were injured, nearly 4,000 were arrested, and hundreds of buildings were destroyed.

Afterward, a state commission concluded that the riots resulted from more complex problems than a simple traffic violation. Rioters were frustrated by the high jobless rate in the inner city, poor housing, and bad schools.

Another issue that heightened racial tensions was an amendment, Proposition 14, to the California Constitution. The amendment said that the state could not interfere with property owners' rights to decide how they rented, leased, or sold their property. The amendment, approved by California voters in 1964, effectively blocked the 1963 Rumford Fair Housing Act, which stated that property owners could not keep "colored" customers from renting or buying their property.

In 1967, the United States Supreme Court ruled that Proposition 14 was unconstitutional. Many saw the court's ruling as a major victory for equal rights in California.

toilets, a hide-a-bed sofa, and running water. Angelou was determined to produce the play herself until she discovered what it would cost. Instead, she decided to move back to New York City.

She had many friends back East. She contacted the Harlem Writers Guild and owners of nightclubs where she once worked. They helped her find an apartment, and gave her furniture and money while she worked on her writing.

A TURBULENT YEAR

For Angelou, 1968 was an earth-shattering year, full of thrilling highs and terrible lows. At a celebration of W.E.B. DuBois's birth, Martin Luther King, Jr., asked Angelou to help the Southern Christian Leadership Conference prepare for a poor people's march on Washington, D.C. He told her, "I'd like each big church to donate one Sunday's collection to the poor people's march. I need you, Maya. Not too many black preachers can resist a good-looking woman with a good idea."

He was well aware of her deeds as an activist. He said, "When someone accuses me of just being nonviolent, I can say ... I've got Maya Angelou back with me."

Angelou agreed to join the cause on her birthday, April 4, but she never got there. King was shot to death that day on a balcony of a motel in Memphis, Tennessee, where he was preparing to lead a march in support of a sanitation workers' strike. She plunged into despair, withdrawing from her friends and remaining in her apartment.

Some time later, her friend James Baldwin insisted that she accompany him to a dinner party given by Jules and Judy Feiffer. Good food and good conversation cheered her, and she entertained the guests with stories. Judy Feiffer called Robert Loomis, a Random House editor, suggesting that Angelou write her life story.

At first, she declined. "I'm pretty certain that I will not write an autobiography," she told him. "I didn't celebrate it, but I have only had my fortieth birthday this year. Maybe in 10 or 20 years."

More to the point, she was writing a 10-part series about African-American culture for a San Francisco public television station. She wanted *Black, Blues, Black* to show the African influence on American poetry, spirituals, ballet, and art.

Nearly dared not to attempt the autobiography, Angelou agreed to try. She holed up in her New York apartment. Her friend Dolly McPherson watched over her. "I had to take it upon myself to see that she was fed," McPherson said. "She would lock the door for days at a time."

Angelou wrote *I Know Why the Caged Bird Sings* with more in mind than simply describing her first 17 years. She said, "I wasn't thinking so much about my own life or identity. I was thinking about a particular time in which I lived and the influences of that time on a number of people.... I used the central figure—myself—as a focus to show how one person can make it through those times."

I Know Why the Caged Bird Sings soared onto the *New York Times* nonfiction bestseller list and stayed there for weeks, making Angelou the first African American to be on the list. It was nominated for a National Book Award.

Loomis, the Random House editor, said, "She wrote with such anger and disgust at the prejudice, but did not have any of the bitterness, which ruins a lot of writers." Critics immediately recognized how Angelou improved the autobiographical style. *Life* magazine called her "a dancer who writes a graceful, pirouetting style that can switch to down-home blues in about one funky second."

"Miss Angelou," the reviewer wrote, "has one fresh and invaluable asset to add to the genre: herself. The Negro woman in autobiography has tended to be formidable ... a dedicated somebody you'd rather revere than meet. Miss Angelou, you would like to meet."

PUBLISHED POET

In 1971, Angelou's first book of poetry, *Just Give Me a Cool Drink of Water 'Fore I Diiie,* was published and nominated for a Pulitzer Prize. One reviewer said that the book was not "accomplished" but "some readers are going to love it." They did. It included some poems originally published as songs in her 1969 recording of *The Poetry of Maya Angelou.* The collection included love poems, which described the happiness of finding love and the pain of losing it. Others were poems of the skin, describing slavery's agonies, the anger of the Watts riots, and war's injustices.

Angelou starts a poem by writing down pages and pages of what she knows about the subject while looking for its rhythm. "Then I start to work on the poem, and I will pull and push it and kick it and kiss it, hug it, everything.... It costs me.

It might take me three months to write that poem. And it might end up being six lines."

"Harlem Hopscotch" showed how Angelou always combines rhythm and theme in a poem. The poem used the unique beat of a sidewalk game while describing triumph over discrimination and life's difficulties.

"You know, all kids when they jump hopscotch, they have a dum-dum-dum, dum-dum-dum rhythm," Angelou explained, "but Harlem's rhythms are a bit different. They're poli-rhythms. So it's dum-dum-dickey-dickey-dum-dum-de-dum."

In 1972, Angelou added another accomplishment to her list of "firsts." Her *Georgia, Georgia* was the first screenplay by an African-American woman to be produced. She had no training in writing music, but she composed its score with a tape recorder. "I'd sing the piano part, sing the first violin part, the second violin, cello, and bass. Then I'd put the whole score in a shopping bag for the transcriber."

Angelou's story is about a black entertainer on tour in Sweden who falls in love with a white photographer. The entertainer's traveling companion, who hates whites, interferes with the two lovers. The entertainer is eventually murdered.

Produced in Sweden by a young Swedish filmmaker, the film received mixed reviews; viewers either liked it very much or hated it very much. Angelou saw it as a learning experience.

In 1973, Angelou returned to the stage to play Mary Todd Lincoln's dressmaker in *Look Away*. Though the play closed on opening night, Angelou received a Tony nomination for her performance.

A NEW HUSBAND

The same year, Angelou was married for a third time, to Paul Du Feu, a white Briton she met at a London dinner party. At first, she worried about the interracial marriage. But her friend James Baldwin told her, "You talk courage, and you encourage us all to dare to love. You love this man and you are questioning ... what?"

They married at the multiracial Glide Memorial Church in San Francisco and settled in Sonoma's Valley of the Moon. For a time they gardened, raising corn, cabbage, lettuce, onions, collard greens, and potatoes to share with their neighbors. Both loved to cook as well.

"My mother says I have married a few times, but this is the first time I've given her a son-in-law," Angelou said shortly after her marriage. "At the ceremony my brother took his glasses off and tears were on his face and said, 'I want to go on record and look Paul Du Feu in the eyes and call him brother.'"

Her life was very busy. Her grandson, Colin Ashanti Murphy-Johnson, was born. Colleges and universities wanted her to speak. After the publication of *I Know Why the Caged Bird Sings*, she received a Yale University fellowship and was appointed writer-in-residence at the University of Kansas. A few years later, she became a distinguished visiting professor at Wake Forest University, Wichita State University, and California State University, Sacramento.

In 1974, Angelou published the second volume of her autobiography, *Gather Together in My Name*. It told of her brushes with prostitution and drugs. She talked about the subject matter with her family before she sent in the manuscript. "My mother said, 'Write it,'" Angelou recalled. "My brother said, 'Send it in.' My son got up ... and reached over and got Paul and me in those massive arms and said, 'You're so great, Mom. Please tell it.'

"I had said, 'People will hate me.'

"[My husband] said, 'Write it if it's true. It's important that you write it.'"

GROWING RECOGNITION

I Know Why the Caged Bird Sings was a hard act to follow. Still, critics were pleased that she had written more about her life. Angelou seemed to alternate between writing her life story and writing poetry. After *Gather Together in My Name*, she published 36 poems in the collection *Oh Pray My Wings Are Gonna Fit Me Well* in 1975. She dedicated it to her husband, Paul Du Feu. President Gerald Ford appointed her to the American Revolution Bicentennial Council. President Jimmy Carter would appoint her to his Presidential Commission for International Women's Year three years later. She wrote six half-hour programs, *Assignment America*, for television.

In 1976, *Singin' and Swingin' and Gettin' Merry Like Christmas*, the third volume of her autobiography, told of her tour with *Porgy and Bess*. The title referred to a time when blacks sang and danced all weekend, stocking up on "good times" so they could live through difficulties the rest of the week. Her mother found long letters that Angelou wrote to her during the tour. They proved Angelou's memory was accurate.

Angelou was chosen as Woman of the Year in Communications by *Ladies' Home Journal*. She finally directed *All Day Long*, the play she had written in California.

Angelou continued to pick up recognition. In 1977, she was nominated for an Emmy Award as Best Supporting Actress for playing Nyo Boto in the TV miniseries *Roots*. Though on screen just a short time, critics remembered her performance

IN HER OWN WORDS...

For Maya Angelou, the process of writing sometimes even turns up in her sleep. She said:

There is a dream which I delight in and long for when I'm writing. It means to me that the work is going well. Or will go well. Or that I'm telling the truth and telling it well.

I dream of a very tall building. It's in the process of being built and there are scaffolds and steps. It looks sort of like the inside of the Arc de Triomphe. I'm climbing it with alacrity and joy and laughter.... I can't tell you how delicious it is.

Maya Angelou appeared at the 1976 taping of the television special for the *Ladies' Home Journal*'s "Woman of the Year." With Angelou were (from left) actress and consumer advocate Betty Furness, early-childhood educator Bettye Caldwell, singer Kate Smith, First Lady Betty Ford, public health activist Dr. Annie D. Wauneka, and Olympic diver Micki King.

as the stern, but loving, grandmother of the young Kunta Kinte. The part brought Angelou further into the public's eye.

"After it was done, I found that people knew me," she said. "I've written five books, I can't say how many plays, movie scripts, music, and poetry, and so forth. I walk down the street and people say, 'You're the actress in *Roots*. What's your name again, and what have you been doing all this time?'"

AND STILL I RISE

In 1978, Angelou published *And Still I Rise*, another volume of poetry. In it, she wrote about her family. Her uncle from Stamps, Arkansas, was the subject of "Willie." She wrote:

Maya Angelou received an Emmy nomination for Best Supporting Actress for her role in the 1977 miniseries _Roots_. Here, she stands behind actress Cicely Tyson. The part brought Angelou even more public recognition.

> Willie was a man without fame,
> Hardly anybody knew his name.
> Crippled and limping, always walking lame,
> He said, "I keep on movin'
> Movin' just the same."*

The title poem is one she uses often in her public readings and lectures. It includes two themes often found in her writing, "the indomitable spirit of the black people" and "the strong, proud female." The last stanza of the poem goes like this:

---

* "Willie," copyright © 1978 by Maya Angelou, from AND STILL I RISE by Maya Angelou. Used by permission of Random House, Inc.

Leaving behind nights of terror and fear
I rise
Into a daybreak that's wondrously clear
I rise
Bringing the gifts that my ancestors gave,
I am the dream and the hope of the slave.
I rise
I rise
I rise.*

Audiences, listening to Angelou recite her poetry, love the poem. They hear her pride in her race and her gender. It is easy to imagine Angelou is talking about herself and all she has experienced.

The 1970s began with the book *I Know Why the Caged Bird Sings*. The decade ended the same. When Angelou adapted the book into a two-hour television movie in 1979, millions more learned her story.

---

* "Still I Rise," copyright © 1978 by Maya Angelou, from AND STILL I RISE by Maya Angelou. Used by permission of Random House, Inc.

8

Dr. Maya Angelou

In 1981, Angelou's life took another series of new directions. She divorced Paul De Feu and moved 3,000 miles to Winston-Salem, North Carolina.

Her association with Wake Forest University began after a campus lecture 10 years before, when students responded enthusiastically to her talk, "Africanisms Still Evident in American Life." Afterward, about 100 students, black and white, peppered her with questions in the student lounge.

"She had the audience so caught up that, by the end of the evening, they were standing up and firing questions at her right and left," said Thomas Mullen, the dean of students. "Usually you have to pry questions out of kids. She opened them up. She made them feel something."

Afterward, Mullen approached Angelou with the job offer. "If you ever want to retire, we offer you a place at Wake Forest. We'd be honored to have you here."

Angelou became the Z. Smith Reynolds Professor of American Studies. She taught a semester course of her own choosing in the field of humanities and then devoted herself to writing. Such appointments are usually for periods of two to five years. Angelou received a lifetime appointment.

"I am a very good teacher," she said. "I will use any ploy to do anything to convey my message. I will sing. I will read Shakespeare.... No one comes to my class on time. They must be early." Her definition of teacher is a good one. "The teacher offers ... ways in which the person can educate himself or herself," she said. "At best the teacher wakes up, shakes up that person, and makes a person hungry."

Her home in Winston-Salem is a beautiful brick structure with a white column porch. Inside, it is decorated with her collection of African and black American art, lush furniture, and the books she loves.

THE HEART OF A WOMAN

Angelou published *The Heart of a Woman,* her fourth volume of autobiography, in 1981. The book's title came from a poem by Georgia Douglas Johnson. In the book, Angelou wrote about what she held dear. It described her involvement in the 1960s civil-rights movement, meeting the militant Malcolm X, the peacemaker Martin Luther King, Jr., and the blues singer Billie Holiday. She wrote of her love affair with Vusumzi Make and her time in Egypt and Ghana.

Angelou, always the adoring mother, recorded Guy's teen years, from age 12 to 18. Except for a year when Angelou toured in Europe and a month when he was kidnapped by Big Mary as an infant, they had been inseparable all his life. Yet, they struggled to get along as he outgrew his childhood games of Scrabble and charades. He took a teenage attitude that household rules were to be obeyed only because "he was just too bored to contest them." The book ended as he recovered from a serious car accident and hurried off to the University of Ghana with new friends.

Critics praised *The Heart of a Woman,* calling it the best of her autobiographies since *I Know Why the Caged Bird Sings.* One critic said it covered "one of the most exciting periods in recent African and Afro-American history." Another said that by "recreating her own experience, she provides a vivid picture of a turbulent time." Still another said that Angelou wrote with such "inner truthfulness that each of her books is a continuing autobiography of Afro-America."

That was exactly what Angelou intended. She often said she described her own life in order to describe the lives of many people, both African American and otherwise. She once said, "I write about the black experience, because it's what I know. But I'm always talking about the human condition, what human beings feel and how we feel."

AT WORK WRITING

Producing autobiographies, poetry, plays, television programs, and speeches required a disciplined writing day. Angelou never writes at home, where cooking, decorations, or telephone calls could be a distraction. Instead, she goes to a hotel room with yellow legal pads, a deck of cards, a Bible, a thesaurus, a dictionary, and a bottle of sherry. There are no pictures on the walls. She will not let the maids clean the room or change the bedsheets. She writes on the bed, leaning on one elbow. Writing in longhand, she works from 6:00 A.M. to mid-afternoon, wearing a hat or tight head tie. "I suppose I hope by doing that I will keep my brains from seeping out of my scalp and running in great gray blobs down my neck, into my ears, and over my face," she said.

Angelou believes daring is as important as discipline. "The person who dares to go out there and test the ledge, that shaky place: that's the artist."

She also cautions that success is never guaranteed. "Not everything you do is going to be a masterpiece," she said. "But you get out there and you really try and sometimes you really do, you write that masterpiece, you sing that classic."

Angelou is irritated by those who think she is a natural writer. "A natural writer!" she said. "And here I've been working maybe two weeks on a single paragraph—a paragraph that nobody's going to notice at all."

Never one to narrow her creativity, Angelou wrote the television movie *Sister, Sister*. The story centered on three sisters who come together after their father's death. The oldest sister wanted to run the trio's lives by a strict moral code; another sister's wild life conflicted with that. The third sister struggled to become independent. The movie aired on NBC in 1982.

In 1983, Angelou published *Shaker, Why Don't You Sing?* She dedicated these poems to her son, Guy Johnson, and her seven-year-old grandson, Colin Ashanti Murphy-Johnson, who had been kidnapped by his mother and remained missing until 1985.

POEMS OF TRIUMPH

Just like her autobiographies, many of the 28 poems in *Shaker, Why Don't You Sing?* described overcoming defeat or despair either in love or in the black struggle against oppression and prejudice. She included a poem, "Caged Bird," that reminded readers of the first volume of her autobiography. In the poem, she described two birds. One was free and flew about "on the back of the wind." The other was trapped by "bars of rage / his wings are clipped and his feet are tied, so he opens his throat to sing." That bird's song was one of freedom. One reviewer, Carol E. Neubauer, said that "as long as such melodies are sung and heard, hope and strength will overcome." The birds in Angelou's poem and her autobiography triumphed.

Angelou may write about serious topics, but she is not always serious. Once, in an interview, she talked about what she would teach her daughter if she had one. Besides learning never to be defeated, she said, "I would teach her to laugh a lot. Laugh a lot at the—at the silliest things and be very, very serious. I'd teach her to love life, I can bet you that."

Critics generally like Angelou's autobiographies better than her poetry. They sometimes think her images are too ordinary. Other experts have criticized her frequent use of rhyme. Still others believe such short poems cannot express complex ideas.

But other critics point out that "a good Angelou poem has ... 'possibilities.'" Some agree that her poems are not really great poems but the public understands and enjoys their images and ideas. As critic Lyman B. Hagen said, "They are written for people, not other poets." He believes that her poems are influenced by the Bible, Shakespeare, Edgar Allan Poe, Langston Hughes, and even the singing in church services.

Angelou's longtime editor, Robert Loomis, thinks that those who do not get her style of poetry do not understand she is writing from a "certain tradition of black American poetry."

"Maya is not writing the sort of poetry that most of us grew up in school admiring," he said. "What she is writing is poetry that ... can be read aloud and even acted. When her words are spoken, they are extremely effective and moving. They always sound just right."

Angelou accepts any criticism with a grain of salt. "I do the best I can with everything. I have no apologies.... I'm holding nothing back."

In 1986, *All God's Children Need Traveling Shoes* was her fifth volume of autobiography. It described her life in Ghana. Wanda Coleman, a *Los Angeles Times* book reviewer, said the book was "an important documentary drawing much more needed attention to the hidden history of a people both African and American."

Just as important, Angelou wrote about her quest, like other black Americans in Africa, to find "home." Though, at first, she thought home was on the continent of her ancestors, she eventually changed her mind. She realized that "home" was not in a geographical location, but in the heart. For her, "home" was centered in her love of her son, Guy. She told an interviewer

Maya Angelou posed for a photograph in 1986 in New York City. That year, her fifth volume of autobiography, *All God's Children Need Traveling Shoes*, was published. The book detailed her life in Ghana in the 1960s and her quest to find a home in Africa.

after the book was published, "The truth is, you can never leave home. You take it with you; it's under your fingernails; it's in the hair follicles; it's in the way you smile."

Angelou tried something new in 1987 with Tom Feelings, a children's book illustrator and two-time Caldecott Medal Honor winner. Feelings, who also lived in Ghana for a time, was looking for a writer who could give words to his drawings. The drawings, of women who "reflect the continent of Africa," had been sketched over 25 years. They captured women in ordinary places, like cafes, nightclubs, and marketplaces. He asked Angelou to write a poem because she had experienced similar situations during her time in Ghana.

Now Sheba Sings the Song was the result. Together, the drawings and the poem celebrated what Feelings said was "Africa's beauty, strength, and dignity [which are] wherever the Black woman is."

In 1988, Angelou continued to be active in the causes she believed in. Her face, her name, and her voice were recognizable to almost everyone—much to her amusement. In Berkeley, California, she and a friend were arrested by an African-American police officer at an anti-apartheid rally. "When she fingerprinted me, her hands were shaking, and she asked me for my autograph," Angelou said.

By 1989, Angelou had been named to *USA Today*'s list of 50 black role models. Reviewers, despite their occasional criticisms of her writing, greatly respect her. One reviewer said that she

DID YOU KNOW?

Did you know that Maya Angelou has been awarded nearly 60 honorary doctorate degrees, but she never went to college? Did you know that Maya Angelou has written 23 books, 6 plays, 2 screenplays, and dozens of magazine articles, but she never enrolled in a writing class? Did you know that Maya Angelou made a living singing but cannot read music?

was becoming a "self-created Everywoman." Another compared her to the legendary Frederick Douglass, saying that "as people who have lived varied and vigorous lives, they embody the quintessential experiences of their race and culture."

9

Cultural Hero

Maya Angelou published another volume of poetry in 1990. *I Shall Not Be Moved* included many topics covered in her other poetry books. It highlighted the many variations of love as well as the many pains of living as a black American.

In "Our Grandmothers," Angelou beautifully described the enduring spirit of black women from slavery to the present:

> She lay, skin down on the moist dirt,
> the canebrake rustling
> with the whispers of leaves, and
> loud longing of hounds and
> the ransack of hunters crackling the near branches.
>
> She muttered, lifting her head a nod toward freedom,
> I shall not, I shall not be moved.*

---

* "Our Grandmothers," copyright © 1990 by Maya Angelou, from I SHALL NOT BE MOVED by Maya Angelou. Used by permission of Random House, Inc.

This volume received high praise. *Publishers Weekly* said that Angelou "writes with poise and grace." *Library Journal,* another respected reviewer, said the book was "an important new collection from one of the most distinct writers at work today." Her publisher, Random House, called the 1990 poems "gems—many-faceted, bright with wisdom, radiant with life."

In 1992, Angelou returned to television. She made *Maya Angelou: Rainbow in the Clouds,* which was shown on PBS. The program focused on Glide Memorial Church in San Francisco. The church was known for its political and social activities fighting hunger, prejudice, and drugs. Angelou was familiar with the church, and had been married there.

Also in 1992, Angelou was the subject of a tribute by the National Society for the Prevention of Cruelty to Children in London. At the March event, the society named the Maya Angelou Child Protection Team and Family Center in her honor.

A MOMENTOUS INVITATION

A phone call on December 1 brought the most important news to America's larger-than-life writer that year. The 64-year-old Angelou was contacted by the co-chairman of the Clinton Inaugural Committee. He told her that President-elect Bill Clinton had personally requested that she write a poem for his swearing-in ceremony. His choice seemed logical. Her writing often described the triumph, hope, and courage of people in overcoming difficult circumstances. One of her poems would set a positive tone for his new administration. Besides, both Clinton and Angelou were raised in Arkansas. His hometown, Hope, is just 25 miles from Stamps, where Maya grew up.

"I didn't take it all in at the time," Angelou said of the invitation. "I was bowled over. I did sit down." Before she started her assignment, she studied the works of the black intellectual W.E.B. DuBois and the poet Frances Ellen Watkins Harper, and the sermons of African-American preachers. She read aloud works by Frederick Douglass, Patrick Henry, and Thomas Paine in her home.

"I can hardly sleep," she told *People Weekly* before the inauguration. "People stop me on the street and in hotel lobbies and say, 'Please say something.' Whites ask, 'Will you please say something to stop the hate?' Black people say, 'Tell our story.' Women … Oooh."

Angelou had only a month to compose the poem. Just as she had done all her life, Angelou holed up in a hotel room away from her 18-room home outside Winston-Salem, North Carolina.

"The writing of poetry is so private, so reclusive, one has to really withdraw inside one's self to a place that is inviolate," Angelou said in an interview for *Ebony* magazine. "But when a whole country knows that you are writing a poem, it is very hard to withdraw. Even on an airplane, people would pass by my seat and say: 'Mornin', finish your poem yet?'"

Angelou wrote down all she could think of about America. From the 200 pages of handwritten ideas, she reduced "On the Pulse of Morning" down to 668 words. It began:

> A Rock, A River, A Tree
> Hosts to species long since departed,
> Marked the mastodon,
> The dinosaur, who left dried tokens
> Of their sojourn here
> On our planet floor,
> Any broad alarm of their hastening doom
> Is lost in the gloom of dust and ages.*

The first line of the poem came from spirituals. "A Rock" came from "No Hiding Place Down Here." "A River" referred to the

---

* From ON THE PULSE OF MORNING by Maya Angelou, copyright © 1993 by Maya Angelou. Used by permission of Random House, Inc.

song, "Deep River." "A Tree" came from her grandmother's favorite song, "I Shall Not Be Moved."

The rest of the poem restated Angelou's favorite themes: that human beings are more alike than they are different and that America should strive for unity and peace. It ended with Angelou's request:

> Here, on the pulse of this new day,
> You may have the grace to look up and out
> And into your sister's eyes,
> And into your brother's face,
> Your country,
> And say simply
> Very simply
> With hope—
> Good morning.*

On a crisp, cold January 20, she stood on the ceremonial balcony in front of the Capitol. Government officials sat behind her, waiting for her message. Thousands in front of her spread out like a fan toward the Washington Monument. Millions more watched on television. She was the first poet to read at an inauguration since Robert Frost recited "The Gift Outright" for John F. Kennedy more than 30 years earlier. She was the first African American and the first woman to do so. After she read "On the Pulse of Morning," President Clinton told her, "I loved your poem," and promised that a copy of it would be placed in the White House.

Rita Dove, a Pulitzer Prize winner in poetry, said of the poem, "It's a song really." The public liked it, too. Angelou said, "People say to me, 'Thank you for our poem.' That's what I wanted." Interest in the poem was so high that her publisher

---

* From ON THE PULSE OF MORNING by Maya Angelou, copyright © 1993 by Maya Angelou. Used by permission of Random House, Inc.

President Bill Clinton reached out to hug Maya Angelou after she delivered her poem "On the Pulse of Morning" at his inauguration on January 20, 1993. After Angelou's address, *I Know Why the Caged Bird Sings* returned to the bestseller list, and sales of her other works rose 600 percent.

released a commemorative edition of the piece. *I Know Why the Caged Bird Sings,* which had sold 2 million copies to that point, jumped back onto the paperback bestseller lists and stayed there for 143 weeks. Sales of her other works jumped 600 percent. She became one of the most sought-after speakers on the lecture circuit. Three full-time assistants helped keep her schedules straight. *I Know Why the Caged Bird Sings* became required reading in some schools.

"I think my delivery [at the inauguration] had its own impact," Angelou said of her increased celebrity. "Before, I could pass 100 people and maybe 10 would recognize me. Now, maybe 40 percent recognize me. If they hear my voice, another 30 percent do, too." In 1994, she won the first of several Grammy Awards for her recording of "On the Pulse of Morning."

LIKE A DAUGHTER

Ever since Martin Luther King, Jr., was killed on her birthday in 1968, Angelou had avoided celebrating on April 4. So, in June 1993, Angelou's good friend Oprah Winfrey held "the mother of all birthday parties" for the 65-year-old Angelou. Winfrey brought in flowers and chefs from all over the world. She even designed the dress Angelou wore. Guy Johnson (Angelou's son), Colin Ashanti Murphy-Johnson (her grandson), and 400 of her friends celebrated on the Wake Forest University campus. President Clinton sent a videotape on which he called her "a treasure to the world."

Angelou first met Winfrey when Winfrey was just getting started in television. Working on a show in Baltimore, Maryland, Winfrey requested a five-minute interview with Angelou. True to her word, Winfrey ended the interview on the dot. Angelou was very impressed. Winfrey felt an immediate connection to Angelou. Both women had been raised in the South by a no-nonsense grandmother. Each woman had been raped as a young child.

Their friendship grew. Angelou invited Winfrey to her home for Winfrey's favorite dish, "smothered chicken dinner." They read poetry in the living room in their pajamas. Angelou often appeared on Winfrey's talk show.

IN HER OWN WORDS...

Maya Angelou, who is much in demand as a speaker, is never at a loss for what to say:

> It's said that a good speaker has four or five different topics but one theme, whether it's furniture building or thermonuclear propulsion. My theme is that human beings are more alike than un-alike. That is my music, my poetry, my films, my plays, my books.

"She has been my counsel, consultant, advisor, shoulder to cry on. Rock. Shield. Protector. Defender. Mama Bear. And Mother-Sister-Friend," Winfrey said.

The feeling is mutual. At her birthday party, Angelou said, "Oprah ... is the kind of daughter I would have wanted to have." She dedicated *Wouldn't Take Nothing for My Journey Now* to Winfrey "with immeasurable love." In this book of essays, she gave advice on travel, jealousy, and brotherhood that all women could appreciate.

WORKS FOR YOUNG READERS

Angelou turned her attention to children's books. In *Life Doesn't Frighten Me,* Jean-Michel Basquiat's drawings and Angelou's words reminded readers of scary things: shadows, noises in the hall, lions on the loose, barking dogs, ghosts, and dragons. Just as in many of her other writings, she told readers that courage would overcome fears.

The book was written for children from four to nine years old, but adults enjoyed it as well. A mother of a seven-year-old wrote to a bookseller, "After reading it, my daughter felt fearless, realizing that she was the master of her emotion and was not at the mercy of 'scary things.'"

One adult liked it for himself. He said, "My advice to parents is this: don't give this book to your kids—buy it for yourselves and keep it someplace where it won't get all trashed up by dirty little hands."

In 1994, another children's book, *My Painted House, My Friendly Chicken, and Me,* introduced Thandi, an eight-year-old girl from an actual Ndebele village in South Africa. Angelou's Thandi described her pet chicken and the decorated houses in her village so that readers could see the culture of the African village. Photographs of the villagers' brilliant beadwork and blankets accompanied the text.

Angelou also received the Springarn Medal, the highest honor awarded by the National Association for the Advancement of

Colored People (NAACP). It is awarded for outstanding achievement by a black American. Winfrey introduced her, and President Clinton called during the ceremonies to congratulate her. "This is the best award that my people could have ever given me," Angelou said.

Angelou branched out into several areas in 1995. She played Anna in the movie *How to Make an American Quilt*, a story about a group of women who talk about their pasts as they sew. Her publisher, Random House, published *Phenomenal Woman: Four Poems Celebrating Women*. She was asked to compose and read a poem for two important events. On July 5, 1995, she read, "A Brave and Startling Truth" for the fiftieth anniversary of the United Nations. Three months later, on October 16, 1995, she

Maya Angelou spoke during the Million Man March, a gathering of more than 500,000 people on October 16, 1995, in Washington, D.C. She was one of the few women to appear at the event.

was one of the few women appearing at the Million Man March in Washington, D.C. The gathering of more than 500,000 men was organized by Louis Farrakhan, the Nation of Islam leader, to inspire black men to take responsibility for themselves and their families. Flooding the National Mall in Washington, the number of attendees surpassed Martin Luther King's famous "I Have a Dream" march from 32 years earlier.

In 1996, Angelou wrote *Kofi and His Magic,* a picture book about a West African boy who uses his imagination to travel to other places. Everyone praised the photographs of West African people who dressed in gold and beautiful kente cloth. Like other Angelou books, reviewers had mixed opinions. Some called it "a winner." Another called it "a flop."

Now famous all over the world, Angelou was appointed by UNICEF as a National Ambassador. She was in such demand at universities and conferences that she earned $2 million in 1996 in speaking fees alone.

After she appeared on *Sesame Street* in 1999, children recognized Angelou in public places. This inspired her to create more books for young readers. "Of course, I won't stop writing poetry or exploring autobiographical forms, but I intend to increase the amount of children's works I do because I see how hungry they are," Angelou said. "And what impresses me about this is that the children are white, Hispanic, Chinese, various races—and they seem to trust me. And I want to parlay that trust into encouraging them to read."

FILM DIRECTING DEBUT

Angelou added to her lists of "firsts" in 1998 when she directed a feature film. *Down in the Delta* starred Alfre Woodard, Wesley Snipes, Esther Rolle, Al Freeman, Jr., Mary Alice, and Loretta Devine.

The 70-year-old Angelou quickly saw similarities between writing and filmmaking. "I came to see the camera as my pen. I just let the 'pen' tell the story," she said.

Angelou said she was drawn to the story "about a family breaking up and coming back together ... a story about a black family which could have been told about an Irish family, or a Jewish family. It could have been done in Canton, Ohio, and Canton, China."

Snipes left an $80 million movie to work with Angelou. He said, "Her life has been such a hodgepodge of everything—she is a true maverick. We knew she would have the sensibility to direct the film, and that she is successful in everything she does."

Still, despite her awards, honorary degrees, her books, and her poetry, Angelou often says her greatest achievement is her son, Guy Johnson. "My son turned out to be magnificent," Angelou said. "He is a joy, a sheer delight. A good human being who belongs to himself." In November 1998, Johnson published his first book, *Standing at the Scratch Line,* a historical thriller with an African-American protagonist.

Angelou ended the decade and the twentieth century with dozens of honorary degrees and awards. Universities from California to Massachusetts, from South Dakota to Florida honored her. In 1999, a *New York Times* article said she was the most requested speaker on college campuses. She was named one of the 100 best writers of the twentieth century by *Writer's Digest,* receiving a Lifetime Achievement Award for Literature. She had come a long way from that little girl who was afraid to cross the railroad tracks into the white section of Stamps, Arkansas.

10

Wise Woman of the World

In the twenty-first century, Maya Angelou became more than just the sum of her parts: autobiographer, activist, poet, performer, celebrity, and counselor to the world. She also became a living legend.

Ebony magazine named her one of the most intriguing blacks in 2000. She joined standouts in all areas of life: Oprah Winfrey, Michael Jordan, Tiger Woods, Sean Combs, Colin Powell, and Clarence Thomas, an associate justice on the U.S. Supreme Court.

In 2000, President Clinton honored her with the National Medal of Arts. It is awarded to people or institutions that bring arts to the general public. The president hugged her and said Angelou "has shown our world the redemptive healing power of art."

The *Washington Post* called her "an elder wise woman," the *New York Times* called her a "cultural diva," the *Atlanta*

Journal-Constitution described her as "wise-woman elder of the human tribe."

HER "MOST DIFFICULT" AUTOBIOGRAPHY

In 2002, Angelou published *A Song Flung Up to Heaven*. Once again, an Angelou book climbed to the *New York Times* best-seller list. It stayed there for five weeks. "This was the most difficult," Angelou said of the sixth volume of her autobiography. Angelou worked for six years to finish the book because it included so many tragic experiences. Sadly, her brother, Bailey, died while she was writing it. "I didn't know how to write it," she said. "I didn't see how the assassination of Malcolm, the Watts riot, the breakup of a love affair, then Martin King, how I could get all that loose with something uplifting in it."

Closer to home, the book told of the difficult times between Angelou and her son, as he matured into an adult. "Teenagers have to break the bond," she said. "They have to say, 'I'm alive. This is my life.' They wrestle and pull loose from the mooring.... I was not easy either, my mom said."

The book began in 1964 as she was about to leave Ghana and ended as she sat down at the kitchen table to write *I Know Why the Caged Bird Sings*. Though her many fans would protest, Angelou believes *A Song Flung Up to Heaven* is the end

IN HER OWN WORDS...

During a speaking engagement at the University of California, Davis, Maya Angelou entertained 3,000 people with her poetry and anecdotes. She never misses an opportunity to inspire the audience to be better people:

Each time you breathe air, you have one more chance to really make a difference in the world, to introduce kindness ... courtesy ... to introduce sweetness.

A drummer greets Maya Angelou in October 2003 before crypts carrying the remains of African Americans were lowered into the African Burial Ground in Lower Manhattan. In 1991, the remains of more than 400 blacks from the seventeenth and eighteenth centuries were discovered in Lower Manhattan. The African Burial Ground was designated a National Historic Landmark in 1993. After much research, the remains were reburied during this Rite of Ancestral Return ceremony.

of her autobiographies. "After that, it would just be writing about writing, which is something I don't want to do," she said.

If the book becomes her last autobiography, its title seems fitting. Angelou took it from Paul Laurence Dunbar's "Sympathy," just as she did her first book's title.

Angelou didn't quit writing, of course. In 2002, she contracted with Hallmark Cards for a line of greeting cards, pillows, and journals called "Maya Angelou's Life Mosaic." Though her book editor thought the venture was beneath her reputation, Angelou overruled him. She believed the cards would expose people who did not ordinarily read books to her thoughts.

Writing "short" was not easy. "I'm obligated to take two to three pages of prose and compress it into two or three sentences," she said. But the effort is worth it for Angelou, who is sometimes called "The People's Poet." She pointed out to critics that Aesop wrote short, witty poems with a single thought, called epigrams, six centuries before Christ's birth and he remains famous.

TIMELESS

Her name fits with the words *woman, writing*, and *race* as easily as fingers on a hand. Any anthology or publication on those subjects will not surprisingly contain a newly created short story, a recent interview, or a forward written by her. It may contain a reprinted excerpt from a poem or from *I Know Why the Caged Bird Sings*.

Angelou's first book showed up on the list of Best Books for Young Adults 1970. Thirty years later, it made the list of 100 All-Star Choices for Teens 2000. Yet it has often topped the lists of books challenged for their content. Angelou's message still disturbs some, who want it removed from a school's curriculum or reading lists.

She often appears as a keynote speaker at university commencements and anniversaries. She sandwiches her message to graduates and students between songs, poetry, and humorous stories.

She lends her name and presence to worthy causes among the several hundred requests she receives each week. She urged African-American women to lead heart-healthy lives. She narrated a 10-movement choral symphony, of which the subject was breast cancer, in Texas. Interested in low-income health care, she visited a Philadelphia hospital. Women's issues, diversity, and racial tolerance will draw her to a stage.

For a kid once all legs and teeth, Angelou is comfortable with the microphone, podium, sequins, and satin. She sings, she lectures, she recites poetry, and she flirts with the audience. They love it.

When she recites "Phenomenal Woman," a poem she included in *And Still I Rise*, she always gets loud applause. Women can see themselves in her words. And they see Angelou there as well. The poem begins:

> Pretty women wonder where my secret lies.
> I'm not cute or built to suit a fashion model's size
> But when I start to tell them,
> They think I'm telling lies.
> I say,
> It's in the reach of my arms,
> The span of my hips,
> The stride of my step,
> The curl of my lips.
> I'm a woman
> Phenomenally.
> Phenomenal woman,
> That's me....*

Her most famous public appearance, President Clinton's inauguration, was a perfect example of her extraordinary talents. Her performance alone inspired listeners. One woman said, "I felt that this woman could have read the side of a cereal box. Her presence was so powerful and momentous, she made it a statement that I was personally longing to see and hear."

Off stage, her voice still compels listening. She credits her son, Guy, for helping her develop her own style. "... I was 6 foot tall and had a very heavy voice and for a small person, who is a foot and half tall, I must have looked like a mountain," Angelou said. "So I was aware of that.... I spoke softly and quietly and moved, hopefully, not too fast so as not to frighten him."

---

* "Phenomenal Woman," copyright © 1978 by Maya Angelou, from AND STILL I RISE by Maya Angelou. Used by permission of Random House, Inc.

What a Dish

Several years after they met, Maya Angelou invited Oprah Winfrey to her home for supper. Angelou prepared smothered chicken and rice. Everyone liked it. They then spent a pleasant evening reciting and reading poetry.

The next morning, Winfrey came down for breakfast. Instead of eggs and bacon or grits and sausage, Winfrey wondered if there was any leftover chicken.

At the table, she asked, "What do you call this dish?"

Angelou said, "That's smothered chicken."

Winfrey said, "No, this is too good for such a simple name. This is suffocated chicken. This chicken never knew what hit it."

In 2004, Angelou published *Hallelujah! The Welcome Table: A Lifetime of Memories With Recipes.* Her dedication reads, "To O, who said she wanted a big, pretty cookbook. Well, honey, here you are." Always an enthusiastic cook, she included directions for making caramel cake, crackling corn bread, pickled pig's feet, Chakchouka (Moroccan Stew), and homemade biscuits among the 100 recipes. Angelou introduced the book's sections with stories of Stamps, of her trip to Italy, and of a dinner Bailey cooked for Guy.

She also wrote a series of picture books for children called *Maya's World.* Each book, *Angelina of Italy, Izak of Lapland, Renée Marie of France,* and *Mikale of Hawaii,* takes readers to another country.

Maya Angelou has always been more than the talent she writes with. True, she was a pioneer in writing autobiographies. She took a form, as Frederick Douglass had tried, and made it into her own. That style forged the way for other writers, black, white, and female, to explore their own truths. She wrote about subjects that few black women wrote about. Her books revealed what it was like living in a certain time in history, how African Americans fit in (or against) white society,

Nigel Hall escorted Maya Angelou during an event on March 28, 2006, at the Clinton Presidential Library in Little Rock, Arkansas. Angelou was at the library as a speaker and to present 10 scholarships to students who attend historically black colleges and universities.

and how Maya Angelou lived in both. As a child, she wished she were someone else. Today, she celebrates who she is. She says, "I'm so glad I'm a black woman, because if I were anything else, I'd be so jealous."

People all over the world admire Maya Angelou for more than her contributions to literature. As one biographer said, "Maya Angelou's life is her poem." Despite the difficulties she described in her books and poetry, one truth shines through. Maya

Angelou was not broken by her circumstances; she triumphed over them. That message inspires. If one person can survive such terrible experiences, others may be able to do the same.

To all women of the world, those of color and those who are not, she says, "To be a woman is to take responsibility for yourself. To be a woman is to work hard, to count on yourself, to owe nothing. It is to hold the reins of your life in your own hands."

Surely, Maya Angelou has done just that.

A Conversation With Maya Angelou at 75

By Lucinda Moore
From Smithsonian Magazine, April 2003

Turning 75 this month, Maya Angelou has led many lives. She is best known as a writer, for her numerous books of poetry and her six poignant memoirs, including the masterful *I Know Why the Caged Bird Sings*. In February [2003], she won a Grammy for the recorded reading of her most recent memoir, *A Song Flung Up to Heaven*. Her works have earned her more than 30 honorary degrees as well as nominations for a National Book Award and a Pulitzer Prize. She wrote "On the Pulse of Morning" for the 1993 swearing-in of President Bill Clinton, becoming only the second poet in U.S. history—Robert Frost was the first, for John F. Kennedy—invited to compose an inaugural poem.

Less well known are Angelou's other lives: as a singer; as a composer; as a dancer in *Porgy and Bess*; as an actor in the Obie-winning play *The Blacks* and in films such as *Calypso Heat Wave* and *How to Make an American Quilt*; as a civil rights worker with Martin Luther King, Jr.; as a journalist in Egypt and Ghana; as a writer for television and Hollywood; as director of the 1998 film *Down in the Delta*. Angelou is the Reynolds Professor of American Studies at North Carolina's Wake Forest University in Winston-Salem. She is constantly on the lecture circuit and a regular guest on talk shows; she recently created a line of greeting cards for Hallmark. And there is little sign of her slowing down.

But when we met recently in her art-filled home in Winston-Salem, it was her family, not her varied career, that she most wanted to discuss. Our conversation often returned to the loved ones who helped her triumph over the tragedies of her childhood and made her believe she could meet whatever challenge life threw in her path.

Her grandmother Annie Henderson was one of the most important, a pious woman who ran a general store in Stamps, Arkansas. Angelou lived most of her childhood with her grandmother, whom she called "Momma." Angelou's sometimes-absentee mother, Vivian Baxter, had a steel will and several careers of her own. She was an inadvertent player in an early, formative trauma in Angelou's life. When Angelou was 8 and briefly living with Baxter in St. Louis, her mother's boyfriend raped Angelou. The man was arrested, convicted and released; soon after, he was found beaten to death. Believing she had caused the killing because she had told of the rape, Angelou refused to speak for several years; only her beloved older brother, Bailey, could coax her to talk. He remained a source of support throughout her life until his death [in 2002]. And there is Angelou's son, Guy Johnson, 57, author of *Echoes of a Distant Summer* and one other novel. He is, she says, her "monument in the world."

MOORE: You've said that society's view of the black woman is such a threat to her well-being that she will die daily unless she determines how she sees herself. How do you see yourself?

ANGELOU: I just received a letter yesterday from the University of Milan. A person is doing a doctoral dissertation on my work. It's called *Sapienza*, which means wisdom. I'm considered wise, and sometimes I see myself as knowing. Most of the time, I see myself as wanting to know. And I see myself as a very interested person. I've never been bored in my life.

MOORE: You have never been bored? How is that possible?

ANGELOU: Oh God, if I were bored, now that would interest me. I'd think, my God, how did that happen and what's going on? I'd be caught up in it. Are you kidding? Bored? I realized when I was about 20 that I would die. It frightened me so. I mean, I had heard about it, had been told and all that, but that

I ... ? [She points at herself and raises her brows as if in disbelief.] It so terrified me that I double-locked the doors; I made certain that the windows were double-locked—trying to keep death out—and finally I admitted that there was nothing I could do about it. Once I really came to that conclusion, I started enjoying life, and I enjoy it very much.

Another occurrence took place at about the same time—maybe about a year later—and the two occurrences liberated me forever. I had two jobs. I was raising my son. We had a tiny little place to live. My mother had a 14-room house and someone to look after things. She owned a hotel, lots of diamonds. I wouldn't accept anything from her. But once a month she'd cook for me. And I would go to her house and she'd be dressed beautifully.

One day after we'd had lunch, she had to go somewhere. She put on silver-fox furs—this was when the head of one fox would seem to bite into the head of the other—and she would wear them with the tails in front; she would turn it around with the furs arching back. We were halfway down the hill and she said, "Baby"—and she was small; she was 5-feet-4½ and I'm 6 foot—"You know something? I think you're the greatest woman I've ever met." We stopped. I looked down at this pretty little woman made up so perfectly, diamonds in her ears. She said, "Mary McLeod Bethune, Eleanor Roosevelt, my mother and you—you are the greatest." It still brings me to te—. [Her eyes tear up.]

We walked down to the bottom of the hill. She crossed the street to the right to get into her car. I continued across the street and waited for the streetcar. And I got onto the streetcar and I walked to the back. I shall never forget it. I remember the wooden planks of the streetcar. The way the light came through the window. And I thought, suppose she's right? She's very intelligent, and she's too mean to lie. Suppose I really am somebody?

Those two incidents liberated me to think large thoughts, whether I could comprehend them or not [she laughs], but to think ...

MOORE: One of your large thoughts must have been about planning to have a diverse life and career. How do you move so easily from one thing to another?

ANGELOU: I have a theory that nobody understands talent any more than we understand electricity. So I think we've done a real disservice to young people by telling them, "Oh, you be careful. You'll be a jack-of-all-trades and a master of none." It's the stupidest thing I've ever heard. I think you can be a jack-of-all-trades and a mistress-of-all-trades. If you study it, and you put reasonable intelligence and reasonable energy, reasonable electricity to it, you can do that. You may not become Max Roach on the drums. But you can learn the drums. I've long felt that way about things. If I'm asked, "Can you do this?" I think, if I don't do it, it'll be ten years before another black woman is asked to do it. And I say, yes, yes, when do you want it? My mom, you know, was a seaman. At one point, I was in Los Angeles. I called her in San Francisco and said, I want to see you, I'm going to New York and I don't know when I'll be back, so let's meet mid-state. She said, "Oh, baby; I wanted to see you, too, because I'm going to sea." I said, going to see what? She said, "I'm going to become a seaman." I said, Mother, really, come on. She said, "No, they told me they wouldn't let women in their union. I told them, 'You wanna bet?' I put my foot in that door up to my hip so women of every color will get in that union, get aboard a ship and go to sea." She retired in 1980, and Asian, white and black women gave a party for her. They called her the mother of the sea.

So, yes, we cripple our children, we cripple each other with those designations that if you're a brick mason you shouldn't love the ballet. Who made that rule? You ever see a person lay bricks? [She moves her hands in a precise bricklaying manner.] Because of the eye and the hands, of course he or she would like to see ballet. It is that precise, that established, that organized, that sort of development from the bottom to the top.

MOORE: Do you resent the fact that your mother wasn't there for much of your childhood?

ANGELOU: Oh, yes. Yes. I was an abandoned child as far as I was concerned, and Bailey also. We didn't hear from her—we heard maybe twice in seven years or something. And then I realized that she was funny and loving and that there are certainly two different kinds of parents. There is the person who can be a great parent of small children. They dress the children in these sweet little things with bows in their hair and beads on their shoestrings and nice, lovely little socks. But when those same children get to be 14 or 15, the parents don't know what to say to them as they grow breasts and testosterone hits the boy. Well, my mom was a terrible parent of young children. And thank God—I thank God every time I think of it—I was sent to my paternal grandmother. Ah, but my mother was a great parent of a young adult.

When she found out I was pregnant, she said, "All right. Run me a bath, please." Well, in my family, that's really a very nice thing for somebody to ask you to do. Maybe two or three times in my life she had asked me to run her a bath. So I ran her a bath and then she invited me in the bathroom. My mother sat down in the bathtub. She asked me, "Do you love the boy?" I said no. "Does he love you?" I said no. "Well, there's no point in ruining three lives. We're going to have us a baby." And she delivered Guy—because she was a nurse, also. She took me to the hospital. It was during one of the Jewish holidays, and my doctor wasn't there. My mother went in, told the nurses who she was, she washed up, they took me into the delivery room. She got up on the table on her knees with me and put her shoulder against my knee and took my hand, and every time a pain would come she'd tell a joke. I would laugh and laugh [she laughs uproariously] and bear down. And she said, "Here he comes, here he comes." And she put her hand on him first, my son. So throughout her life she liberated me.

Liberated me constantly. Respected me, respected what I tried to do, believed in me. I'd go out in San Francisco—I'd be visiting her, I was living in Los Angeles—and stay really late at some after-hours joint. Mother knew all of them and knew all the bartenders. And I'd be having a drink and laughing, and the bartender would say on the phone, "Yeah, Mama, yeah she's here." She'd say to me: "Baby, it's your mother. Come home. Let the streets know you have somewhere to go."

MOORE: It seems your mother and Bailey always came to your rescue. Were they more vigilant, do you think, because you didn't speak for so long?

ANGELOU: All those years ago I'd been a mute, and my mother and my brother knew that in times of strife and extreme stress, I was likely to retreat to mutism. Mutism is so addictive. And I don't think its powers ever go away. It's as if it's just behind my view, just behind my right shoulder or my left shoulder. If I move quickly, it moves, so I can't see it. But it's always there saying, "You can always come back to me. You have nothing to do—just stop talking." So, when I've been in stress, my mother or my brother, or both sometimes, would come wherever I was, New York, California, anywhere, and say, "Hello, hello, talk to me. Come on, let's go. We'll have a game of Scrabble or pinochle and let's talk. Tell me a story." Because they were astute enough to recognize the power of mutism, I finally was astute enough to recognize the power of their love.

MOORE: What went through your mind during the years you were mute?

ANGELOU: Oh, yes, I memorized poetry. I would test myself, memorizing a conversation that went by when I wasn't in it. I memorized 60 Shakespearean sonnets. And some of the things I memorized, I'd never heard them spoken, so I memorized them according to the cadence that I heard in my head. I loved Edgar Allan Poe and I memorized everything I could find. And I loved Paul Laurence Dunbar—still do—so I would memorize 75 poems. It was like putting a CD on. If I wanted to, I'd just run through my memory and think, that's one I want to hear. So I believe that my brain reconstructed itself during those years. I believe that the areas in the brain which provide and promote physical speech had nothing to do. I believe that the synapses of the brain, instead of just going from A to B, since B wasn't receptive, the synapses went from A to R. You see what I mean? And so, I've been able to develop a memory quite unusual, which has allowed me to learn languages, really quite a few. I seem to be able to direct the brain; I can say, do that. I say, remember this, remember that. And it's caught!

[She snaps her fingers as if to emphasize "caught."]

MOORE: You lived with your grandmother during your silent years. How did she respond?

ANGELOU: She said, "Sister, Momma don't care what these people say; that you must be an idiot, a moron, 'cause you can't talk. Momma don't care. Momma know that when you and the good Lord get ready, you gon' be a teacher."

MOORE: If your mother liberated you to think big, what gifts did your grandmother give you?

ANGELOU: She gave me so many gifts. Confidence that I was loved. She taught me not to lie to myself or anyone else and not to boast. She taught me to admit that, to me, the emperor has no clothes. He may be dressed in the finery of the ages to everybody else, but if I don't see it, to admit that I don't see it. Because of her, I think, I have remained a very simple woman. What you see is all there is. I have no subterfuge. And she taught me not to complain. My grandmother had one thing that she would do for me about twice a year. Shall I tell you? [She laughs loudly.] Momma would see a whiner, a complainer come down the hill. And she would call me in. She'd say; "Sister, Sister, come out here." I'd go and look up the hill and a complainer was trudging. And the man or woman would come into the store, and my grandmother would ask, "How you feel today?" "Ah, Sister Henderson, I tell you I just hate the winter. It makes my face crack and my shins burn."

And Momma'd just say, "Uh-huh," and then look at me. And as soon as the person would leave, my grandmother would say, "Sister, come here." I'd stand right in front of her. She'd say, "There are people all over the world who went to sleep last night who did not wake again. Their beds have become their cooling boards, their blankets have become their winding sheets. They would give anything for just five minutes of what she was complaining about."

MOORE: Did you write during your childhood?

ANGELOU: Well, I've always written. There's a journal which I kept from about 9 years old. The man who gave it to me lived across the street from the store and kept it when my grandmother's papers were destroyed. I'd written some essays. I loved poetry, still do. But I really, really loved it then. I would write some—of course it was terrible—but I'd always written something down.

MOORE: I read that you wrote the inaugural poem, "On the Pulse of Morning," in a hotel room. Were you on the road when you composed it?

ANGELOU: I keep a hotel room here in Winston when I'm writing. I take a room for about a month. And I try to be in the room by 6 A.M., so I get up, make coffee and keep a thermos and I go out to the hotel. I would have had everything removed from the room, wall hangings and all that stuff. It's just a bed, a table and a chair, Roget's Thesaurus, a dictionary, a bottle of sherry, a yellow pad and pens, and I go to work. And I work 'til about twelve or one; one if it's going well, twelve if it isn't. Then I come home and pretend to operate in the familiar, you know?

MOORE: Where does writing rank in your accomplishments?

ANGELOU: I'm happy to be a writer, of prose, poetry, every kind of writing. Every person in the world who isn't a recluse, hermit or mute uses words. I know of no other art form that we always use. So the writer has to take the most used, most familiar objects—nouns, pronouns, verbs, adverbs—ball them together and make them bounce, turn them a certain way and make people get into a romantic mood; and another way, into a bellicose mood. I'm most happy to be a writer.

Reprinted with permission from SMITHSONIAN Magazine (April 2003).

Selected Works by Maya Angelou

AUTOBIOGRAPHIES

I Know Why the Caged Bird Sings (1970)

Gather Together in My Name (1974)

Singin' and Swingin' and Gettin' Merry Like Christmas (1976)

The Heart of a Woman (1981)

All God's Children Need Traveling Shoes (1986)

A Song Flung Up to Heaven (2002)

Hallelujah! The Welcome Table: A Lifetime of Memories With Recipes (2004)

PERSONAL ESSAYS

Wouldn't Take Nothing for My Journey Now (1993)

Even the Stars Look Lonesome (1997)

CHILDREN'S BOOKS

Life Doesn't Frighten Me (1993)

My Painted House, My Friendly Chicken, and Me (1994)

Kofi and His Magic (1996)

Maya's World: Angelina of Italy (2004)

Maya's World: Izak of Lapland (2004)

Maya's World: Mikale of Hawaii (2004)

Maya's World: Renée Marie of France (2004)

POETRY

Just Give Me a Cool Drink of Water 'Fore I Diiie (1971)

Oh Pray My Wings Are Gonna Fit Me Well (1975)

And Still I Rise (1978)

Shaker, Why Don't You Sing? (1983)

Now Sheba Sings the Song (1987)

I Shall Not Be Moved (1990)

"On the Pulse of Morning" (1993)

The Complete Collected Poems of Maya Angelou (1994)

Phenomenal Woman: Four Poems Celebrating Women (1995)

Black Pearls: The Poetry of Maya Angelou (1998)

FILMS AND TELEVISION

Black, Blues, Black (1968) (TV), writer and producer

Georgia, Georgia (1972), writer

Roots (1977) (TV), portraying Nyo Boto

Sister, Sister (1982) (TV), writer

How to Make an American Quilt (1995), portraying Anna

How Do You Spell God? (1996) (TV), writer

Down in the Delta (1998), director

1928 Born April 4 as Marguerite Ann Johnson in St. Louis

1931 Moves to Stamps, Arkansas, with her brother, Bailey

1935 Moves to St. Louis; is raped by mother's boyfriend

1941 Moves to San Francisco to live with her mother

1943 Becomes San Francisco's first African-American street-car conductor

1945 Graduates from high school; gives birth to Clyde Bailey "Guy" Johnson

1950 Marries Tosh Angelos

1952 Divorces Tosh Angelos

1953 Entertains at the Purple Onion nightclub; takes the name Maya Angelou

1954 Joins *Porgy and Bess* touring company in Europe

1959 Moves to New York and joins the Harlem Writers Guild

1960 Meets the Reverend Dr. Martin Luther King, Jr.; marries Vusumzi Make

1961 Moves to Cairo, Egypt; works as an associate editor for the *Arab Observer*

1962 Moves with her son to Accra, Ghana; Guy is injured in an automobile accident; is employed at the University of Ghana

1964 Meets with Malcolm X in Ghana

1965 Returns to the United States to work for Malcolm X; he is assassinated two days after she arrives in the United States

1969 Records *The Poetry of Maya Angelou*

1970 Publishes *I Know Why the Caged Bird Sings*, which is nominated for a National Book Award

1971 Publishes *Just Give Me a Cool Drink of Water 'Fore I Diiie*, which is nominated for a Pulitzer Prize

1972 Is the first African-American woman to have a screenplay (*Georgia, Georgia*) produced

1973 Receives a Tony Award nomination for her performance as Mary Todd Lincoln's dressmaker in *Look Away*; marries Paul Du Feu

1974 Publishes *Gather Together in My Name*; becomes a distinguished visiting professor at Wake Forest University, Wichita State University, and California State University, Sacramento

1975 Publishes *Oh Pray My Wings Are Gonna Fit Me Well*; is selected as a Rockefeller Foundation Scholar

1976 Publishes *Singin' and Swingin' and Gettin' Merry Like Christmas*; is chosen as Woman of the Year in Communications by *Ladies' Home Journal*; directs her play *All Day Long*

1977 Is nominated for an Emmy Award for her role as Kunta Kinte's grandmother in the TV miniseries *Roots*

1978 Publishes *And Still I Rise*

1979 Writes television version of *I Know Why the Caged Bird Sings*

1981 Publishes *The Heart of a Woman*; divorces Paul De Feu; is named Z. Smith Reynolds Professor of American Studies at Wake Forest University

1982 Writes TV movie *Sister, Sister* for NBC

1983 Publishes *Shaker, Why Don't You Sing?*

1986 Publishes *All God's Children Need Traveling Shoes*

1987 Publishes *Now Sheba Sings the Song* with Tom Feelings

1990 Publishes *I Shall Not Be Moved*

1993 Reads "On the Pulse of Morning" at President Bill Clinton's inauguration; publishes *Wouldn't Take Nothing for My Journey Now*; publishes *Life Doesn't Frighten Me*

1994   Publishes *My Painted House, My Friendly Chicken, and Me,* and *The Complete Collected Poems of Maya Angelou*; receives the Springarn Medal, the NAACP's highest honor

1995   Publishes *Phenomenal Woman: Four Poems Celebrating Women*; reads her "A Brave and Startling Truth" at the fiftieth anniversary of the United Nations; reads her "From a Black Woman to a Black Man" at the Million Man March in Washington D.C.

1996   Publishes *Kofi and His Magic*; is appointed as UNICEF's National Ambassador

1997   Publishes *Even the Stars Look Lonesome*

1998   Publishes *Black Pearls: The Poetry of Maya Angelou*; directs *Down in the Delta*

1999   Is named one of the best writers of the twentieth century by *Writer's Digest*

2000   Is presented the National Medal of Arts by President Clinton

2004   Publishes *Hallelujah! The Welcome Table: A Lifetime of Memories With Recipes*

Courtney-Clarke, Margaret. *Maya Angelou: The Poetry of Living.* New York: Clarkson-Potter, 1999.

Cuffie, Terrasita A. *The Importance of Maya Angelou.* San Diego: Lucent Books, 1999.

Harper, Judith E. *Maya Angelou: Journey to Freedom.* Chanhassen, MN: The Child's World Inc., 1999.

Hunter, Shaun. *Writers (Women in Profile).* New York: Crabtree Publishing Company, 1998

Kirkpatrick, Patricia. *Maya Angelou.* Mankato, MN: Creative Education, 2003.

Lisandrelli, Elaine Slivinski. *Maya Angelou: More Than a Poet.* Berkeley Heights, NJ: Enslow Publishers, Inc., 1996.

Pettit, Jayne. *Maya Angelou: Journey of the Heart.* New York: Lodestar Books, 1996.

Strickland, Michael R. *African-American Poets.* Berkeley Heights, NJ: Enslow Publishers, Inc., 1996.

WEBSITES

The Academy of American Poets: Maya Angelou
www.poets.org/poet.php/prmPID/87

Maya Angelou: Chronological chart of her life
www.nwhp.org/tlp/biographies/angelou/angelou_bio.html

Maya Angelou: The official Website
www.mayaangelou.com

Poems by Maya Angelou
www.poemhunter.com/maya-angelou/poet-6834/

Voices from the Gaps biography on Maya Angelou
http://voices.cla.umn.edu/vg/Bios/entries/angelou_maya.html

Picture Credits

Vicki Cox has an M.S. in education and taught in the public school system for 25 years. She writes for national magazines and newspapers in 17 states. She has written eight biographies for children and has authored an anthology that profiles people and places on the Ozark Plateau.